HOW TO WRITE A NOVEL

AND WAYS TO MAKE IT A BEST SELLER

ED ADAMS

A FIRSTELEMENT PRODUCTION

Ed Adams

Published in Great Britain in 2024 by firstelement

Directed by the six twenty

10 9 8 7 6 5 4 3

A CIP catalogue record for this book is available from the British Library.

ISBN: 978-1-913818-55-5

Ebook ISBN: 978-1-913818-56-2

Ed Adams

an imprint of firstelement.co.uk

rashbre@mac.com

ed-adams.net

For Mum

turn, settings that transport. We'll look at the tools and techniques used by both the literary greats and modern storytellers to captivate readers.

Let me introduce myself. I'm someone who's passionate about storytelling and helping others find their voice. I've spent years working with writers, guiding them through the challenges of putting thoughts to paper. I'm committed to providing guidance that's easy to understand and put into practice.

This book is for you—adults and aspiring writers ready to dive into the thrilling world of novel writing. You're eager to learn, improve, and ultimately create a bestseller. Whether you're starting from scratch or looking to refine your craft, you share the dream of seeing your book in readers' hands.

Here's how we'll get there: The book is structured into key chapters, each designed to build on the last. We'll start with plot development, where you'll learn to weave a story that keeps readers hooked from start to finish. Then, we move on to character creation, where we'll craft characters so real they almost leap off the page. We'll delve into worldbuilding, constructing vivid settings that pull readers into your story's universe. Finally, we'll explore marketing strategies to help you navigate the publishing world.

A toolkit of skills

By the end of this book, you'll have a toolkit full of skills. You'll learn to create compelling plot arcs, develop characters that resonate, and conquer writer's block. You'll understand your publishing options, whether you aim for traditional routes or self-publishing. Most importantly, you'll walk away inspired and equipped to tackle your novel-writing journey, no matter what stage you're at.

Planner or Pantser?

It is often described that novelists are either planners or pansters. They plan the entire novel, or they 'fly by the seat of their pants'. Don't worry, either way this book is for you. Either use it as an 'idea to manuscript' resource or for 'dipping in' to find your way through particular situations. Keep it on your desk.

Invitation

So, I invite you to take the first step. Embrace this adventure with confidence and creativity. Turn the page, and let's start this journey together. Read the book once, and you'll have plenty of inspiration. I've made the contents section a kind of buzzword refresher. Then keep the book handy, flick it open and dive in.

It's time to bring your story to life and share it with the world.

CHAPTER 1

LAYING THE FOUNDATION

FOUNDATIONS

There's a moment every writer dreams about. You're sitting in a cosy nook, a cup of something warm by your side, and you finally flip through the last page of your manuscript. It's done, complete, a labour of countless hours and imagination.

You feel a deep sense of accomplishment, a quiet joy that echoes the journey you've taken through characters, worlds, and emotions. But before you reach this moment, there's the groundwork to be laid. Every great novel starts with a solid foundation, and that begins with understanding your writing vision. It's about knowing why you're writing and what you want to say. This chapter is designed to help you sort through these questions and set a sturdy base for your writing adventure.

CRAFTING YOUR WRITING VISION

Core message and purpose

Let's start with the heart of your story—your core message and purpose. Imagine your novel as a conversation with readers. What do you want to say? What feeling or truth do you hope to impart? Crafting a vision statement for your novel can help crystallize these ideas.

A vision statement is like a beacon guiding your writing decisions. It serves as a reminder of the overarching themes and messages you aim to explore. Spend some time reflecting on this. Jot down thoughts, words, or even phrases that capture the essence of your novel. This exercise will not only clarify your intent but also keep you focused when the writing process gets challenging.

Next, let's identify what has shaped your desire to write. Our influences are often a patchwork of personal experiences, cultural backgrounds, and the authors who've inspired us. Consider what events or experiences have left a mark on you. Perhaps a family story, a cultural tradition, or even a moment of personal growth has fuelled your storytelling.

Reflect on these influences and think about how they can be woven into your narrative. Similarly, consider your favourite authors and genres. What draws you to them? Is it the way they craft characters, their use of language, or the themes they explore? Analysing these elements can offer insights into your own writing preferences and help you develop a style that's uniquely yours.

Envision the end product

Now, let's take a moment to envision the end product. Picture your novel sitting on a shelf or in someone's hands. What do you want readers to feel or think after reading it? Visualizing the finished book can provide motivation and direction. It helps you see the bigger picture and understand the impact you wish to have on your audience. This vision can serve as a guiding light during the writing process, reminding you of the ultimate goal.

Long term creative goals

Finally, establish long-term creative goals. Writing a novel is a marathon, not a sprint, and setting milestones can keep you motivated and focused. Break down the writing process into stages, such as completing a first draft, revising, and preparing for publication. Plan for what's next, whether it's launching your book, connecting with readers, or even starting a new project. Having these goals in place will help maintain your momentum and provide a sense of direction.

REFLECTION EXERCISE

Take a moment to write down your vision statement.

- What themes or messages do you want to explore?
- List any personal influences or favourite authors that inspire you?
- Visualize the finished product and note what you hope readers will take away from it. Finally, outline some long-term creative goals for your writing journey.

Keep this reflection handy as a reminder of your purpose and passion.

EXAMPLE NOVEL STRUCTURE

An example of a novel structure is below. It can be used for adventure, fantasy, spy novels, science fiction, crime, romance and many others. Use it as a rough signposting throughout the novel writing process, and don't be afraid to veer away from the conventional path.

Of course, there is no secret sauce to making the perfect novel, but sometimes a few key ingredients can add the right flavours.

STRUCTURE: PART ONE / ACT 1

Hook

The story opens with an engaging scene or line, immediately capturing the reader's attention and setting the tone.

Set-up (1%-12%)

Key details about the characters, their goals, and the stakes are revealed, establishing the story's foundation.

Inciting Event (12%)

A major turning point disrupts the protagonist's ordinary world, serving as a call to adventure and initiating the primary conflict.

Build-Up (12%-25%)

Tension escalates as the groundwork for the central conflict is laid, positioning the necessary elements for the story to unfold.

First Plot Point (25%)

The protagonist steps through the doorway into the second act, leaving the familiar world behind and fully committing to the story's central journey.

By defining your narrative arc and understanding the motivations driving your characters, you create a strong framework for a compelling story. This foundation will not only guide your writing process but also ensure a meaningful and engaging journey for your readers.

STRUCTURE: PART TWO/ACT 2

Reaction (25%-37%)

The protagonist struggles to grasp the challenges posed by the antagonist and begins to navigate this new reality.

1st Pinch Point (37%)

A stark reminder of the antagonist's strength, offering new insights into the conflict and raising the stakes.

Realization (37%-50%)

The protagonist starts to see the bigger picture,, shifting from reactive to more deliberate responses.

Midpoint (50%)

The protagonist discovers a key truth, altering their perspective and strategy.

Action (50%-62%)

With new insight, the protagonist takes bold steps, gaining ground against the antagonist.

2nd Pinch Point (62%)

Foreshadows the third plot point, reinforcing the stakes and risks ahead.

Action (62%-75%)

The protagonist intensifies their efforts, making significant progress against the antagonist and achieving what seems to be a victory.

PART THREE / ACT 3

3rd Plot Point (75%)

The protagonist faces their darkest moment. After achieving a significant victory at the end of Act Two, the tides turn against them in a sudden, devastating reversal.

Recovery (75%-88%)

Struggling to regain their footing, the protagonist is consumed by self-doubt, questioning their decisions, dedication to their goal, and even their own abilities.

Climax Begins (88%)

A critical turning point forces an inevitable confrontation between the protagonist and the antagonist, setting the stage for their final showdown.

Confrontation (88%-98%)

The ultimate clash unfolds—whether literal or metaphorical—a battle where neither the protagonist nor the antagonist can emerge unscathed or unchanged. Only one will prevail.

Climactic Moment (98%)

The protagonist's goal is realized, bringing the central conflict to an irreversible conclusion. Continuing the struggle becomes physically or logically impossible.

Resolution (98%-100%)

Guide readers gently away from the intensity of the climax, providing closure and leaving them with the story's final emotional resonance.

UNDERSTANDING YOUR AUDIENCE

The secret map

Knowing your audience is like having a secret map to guide your writing. It's about understanding who will pick up your book and why they will keep turning the pages. Start by considering the demographic details—age, interests, and reading habits of your potential readers. Are they young adults drawn to fantasy adventures or mature readers who enjoy historical fiction? You can gather this information through surveys, tapping into online communities, or simply engaging in conversations with readers. Look at the books that sit next to yours on the shelf. Analyse their audiences and think about what makes those readers tick. This isn't just about numbers and data; it's about connecting with the people who will love your stories.

Genre Expectations

Expectations are key. Readers come to a genre with certain expectations, and understanding these can help shape your narrative. Dive into reviews and reader forums to see what people are saying about books similar to yours. What excites them? What disappoints them? These insights can help you tailor your content to meet their desires while still keeping your unique voice. It's not about changing your story to fit a mould but rather enhancing your narrative to resonate deeply with those who seek your kind of storytelling. Imagine you're throwing a party. You'd want to know if your guests prefer jazz or rock 'n' roll, right? It's the same with writing.

Dancing with the readers

Adapting your story to your audience doesn't mean losing yourself in the process. Think of it as a dance—finding a rhythm that allows your voice to shine while engaging your readers. Consider the themes and messages that speak to them and see how they align with your narrative. If you're writing a mystery, your readers might crave twists and turns. If it's romance, they might look for emotional depth. Anticipate their needs and weave them into your plot and characters. But remember, authenticity is key. Readers can spot when a story tries too hard to please. Your voice is your fingerprint on the page; it's what makes your story yours.

Criticism is your friend

Criticism and questions are inevitable, but they can be your greatest tool. Think ahead about the objections or concerns readers might have. Are there common tropes in your genre that readers are tired of? Be aware of these pitfalls and consider how you can approach them with fresh eyes. Addressing potential criticisms in advance shows respect for your audience and elevates your writing. It's like being a chef who knows the perfect seasoning to bring out the best flavours, even in a familiar dish. This preparation not only strengthens your story but also builds trust with your readers. They'll appreciate the thoughtfulness behind your words.

Understanding your audience is a bit like learning a new language. It takes time, patience, and a willingness to listen. But once you do, it opens up a world of possibilities for your writing. You start to see the connections between your story and those who will read it, creating a bridge between your imagination and their reality. This connection is what makes your work not just a book but an experience. An experience that invites them to think, feel, and share in the world you've created.

SETTING REALISTIC WRITING GOALS

Chopping down the mountain

Writing a novel can feel like staring at a mountain that needs climbing. The peak might seem distant and daunting, but breaking down the climb into manageable steps can make the ascent feel not only possible but exhilarating. Start by creating a detailed project timeline. This isn't just a schedule; it's your roadmap. Consider the stages of writing—outlining, drafting, revising. Assign realistic timeframes to each phase, allowing for life's interruptions. Then, set daily or weekly word count targets. These targets should challenge you but not overwhelm you. If you're new to writing, maybe 300 words a day feels right. More seasoned? Perhaps 1,000 words. The key is consistency over quantity. Tracking these small increments will eventually lead you to a completed manuscript, much like stitching together patches of fabric into a quilt.

Be SMART, not vague

To make your goals effective, use the SMART criteria: Specific, Measurable, Achievable, Relevant, and Time-bound. This approach provides clarity and direction. Instead of vague aspirations like "finish my novel," try "write 10,000 words by the end of the month." This specificity makes it easier to measure progress and know when you've hit your mark. It's important that your goals are realistic, given your resources and time. Writing a novel while juggling a full-time job or family responsibilities requires goals that fit into your life, not disrupt it. Make sure your writing goals align with what you want to achieve in your life and career. If your writing is a passion project, the goals might differ from those of someone pursuing a full-time writing career. Time-bound goals help keep the pressure constructive, setting a deadline to work towards without making it feel like a looming threat.

Monitor

Monitoring your progress is crucial. It allows you not just to track how far you've come but also to make necessary adjustments. Consider using tracking tools or progress journals. These can be as simple as a spreadsheet marking daily word counts or as elaborate as a bullet journal filled with colour-coded milestones. Regular reviews of your progress help identify patterns—perhaps you write best in the mornings, or maybe your word count dips on weekends. Use this insight to adapt your timeline or targets, ensuring they remain both challenging and feasible. Remember, flexibility is not a sign of failure but a tool for success. Adjusting goals in response to real-life circumstances keeps the writing process sustainable and enjoyable.

Yay! Celebrate

Celebrating small victories is often overlooked, yet it is vital for maintaining motivation. Writing a novel is a long-term commitment, and acknowledging small achievements along the way sustains your enthusiasm. Finished a chapter? Treat yourself to something special. Hit your word count for the week? Share the achievement with a friend or writing group. These celebrations reinforce progress, making the process rewarding and less solitary. They serve as a reminder of what you've accomplished and what you're capable of. Much like climbers who pause to admire the view from a new height, taking time to celebrate provides perspective and encouragement for the path ahead.

Manageability

Setting realistic goals transforms the abstract notion of writing a novel into a structured and approachable endeavour. It shifts the focus from the intimidating notion of finishing a book to the tangible act of writing a bit each day. This approach not only makes the task manageable but also aligns with your lifestyle and aspirations. As you traverse the path of writing, these goals serve as both guiding stars and resting points, ensuring you not only reach the end but do so with joy and fulfilment in the craft.

BUILDING A WRITING ROUTINE

Create your writing space

Writers need a space that's conducive to productivity. Because everyone is different, this will vary from writer to writer.

Much is written about writers and their writing spaces, because they can massively impact the writer's productivity. Whether simply rooting out noisy distractions, or meticulously manufacturing that specific yet indescribable ambience, many will work hard to create their perfect writing environment. As Virginia Woolf famously described it ' A room of one's own.'

Craft a routine

Creating a writing routine is like crafting a recipe that suits your tastes, one that nourishes your creativity and fits into your life. It starts with identifying those golden hours when your mind is sharpest, and your ideas flow freely. For some, it might be the quiet calm of early morning before the world stirs and responsibilities creep in. Others might find their muse visits in the dead of night when the silence is thick, and thoughts can meander without interruption. Pinpoint these peak productivity times, and you'll find that writing becomes less of a chore and more of a pleasure.

Lose the distractions

Once you've identified when you're most productive, the next step is to create a writing environment that minimizes distractions. Picture your workspace as a sanctuary for ideas. This might mean clearing away clutter or ensuring that your phone is on silent. Some find solace in a tidy desk, while others thrive amidst organized chaos. Whatever your preference, the goal is to create a space that invites focus and creativity. If you share your space, communicate your needs with those around you, setting boundaries to protect your writing time. Remember, your environment can either invite creativity or stifle it, so make it work for you.

It is important to maintain the flow states we all seek, where ideas come easily and words arrive on the page as if inspired by a higher source. It's equally important to allow uninterrupted thinking, enabling thoughts to explore, imagine, and develop.

Avoiding distractions is essential, especially in today's interconnected world, filled with the demands of work, family, friends, pets, and daily chores. Therefore, it's important to create or find a distraction-free space.

In addition to finding a suitable environment, communicate with your friends and family that when you are in this space (or during specific times) you would prefer not to be disturbed. This way, you can work without the anxiety of being interrupted, allowing you to focus better and nurture your creativity.

Flexibility

Flexibility is key in any routine, especially a writing one. Life is unpredictable, and clinging too rigidly to a schedule can lead to frustration. Allow yourself the grace to adapt. Plan for off-days when the words just won't come and give yourself permission to take breaks. These breaks can be restorative, offering new perspectives and renewed energy when you return to the page. It's like giving your creative muscles a chance to rest before the next workout. Knowing you can adjust your schedule without guilt allows your writing to become a natural part of your life, not an obligation that looms over you.

In our digital age, there are countless tools and resources designed to enhance productivity. Writing software like Scrivener can help organise your thoughts and structure your novel. Its features are designed to streamline the process, allowing you to focus on storytelling rather than technicalities. Time management techniques, like the Pomodoro Technique, can also be invaluable. Work in focused bursts of activity, followed by short breaks, to maintain concentration and prevent burnout. These tools are like having a personal assistant, helping you keep track of time and progress and ensuring that your writing remains both productive and enjoyable.

Rituals, but without the faff

Establishing rituals can be a powerful way to signal to your brain that it's time to write. These rituals act as a bridge, transitioning you from daily life to the creative mindset needed for writing. Maybe it's listening to a specific playlist that stirs your imagination, the familiar tunes guiding you into the narrative world. Or perhaps it's engaging in a pre-writing exercise, like free writing or mind-mapping, to prime your creativity. Some writers find that lighting a candle or sipping a favourite tea becomes a cue that it's time to let the words flow. These rituals, no matter how small, create a sense of anticipation and readiness, making the act of writing feel like a special, intentional part of your day.

Building a writing routine is about finding what works for you and making it a habit.

Comfort

Transforming writing from a simple task into a beloved practice is all about consistency, flexibility, and a sprinkle of ritual! By establishing a rhythm that sparks your creativity, you can seamlessly weave writing into your life, allowing you to not just write, but truly revel in the joy of bringing your stories to life. Creating a cozy and inviting desk setup is essential.

A comfortable workspace not only keeps distractions at bay but also supports your health by reducing the risk of strain injuries and back pain. When your environment feels good, you'll find yourself more eager to dive in regularly.

Remember, while a nurturing writing space is important, the beauty of writing is that you can do it anywhere! Embrace the freedom to write without constraints. Whether you cherish the tranquillity of your shed or discover inspiration in buzzing cafes or on a train, every location has potential. So go ahead, explore the world, and let your creativity flow wherever you are!

OVERCOMING INITIAL WRITING FEARS

Standing at the crossroads

At some point, every writer stands at the crossroads of fear and creativity. It's a familiar place where the echoes of doubt can drown out the call of inspiration. Perhaps you're worried that your writing won't measure up, or that criticism will sting more than you can bear. These fears are not unique—they're part of the writer's landscape. Recognising them is the first step toward quieting them. You might fear failure, the idea that your work won't be well-received or you might not even see the light of day. Or perhaps it's the fear of judgment that others will scrutinise your words, finding them lacking. Acknowledging these fears doesn't mean they have power over you. Instead, it means you're ready to face them head-on, equipped with strategies to manage them.

Anxiety

Managing anxiety in writing requires a toolkit of techniques designed to build confidence and calm the mind. Visualisation exercises can be incredibly practical. Picture yourself at your writing desk, words flowing effortlessly, the story unfolding just as you imagined. This mental rehearsal can create a sense of familiarity and ease when you sit down to write. Alongside visualization, mindfulness practices offer a sanctuary from anxiety. Simple breathing techniques, like deep, measured inhales and exhales, help ground you in the present moment. This focus can dispel the swirling thoughts of doubt, leaving room for creativity to breathe. These methods aren't just about relaxation; they're about transforming your writing space—mentally and physically—into a place of peace and productivity.

Reframing

Fear, surprisingly, can be a potent motivator if you learn to reframe it. Instead of seeing fear as a barrier, view it as a sign that you're pushing boundaries. Let it fuel your determination to prove yourself wrong, to show that those fears are nothing more than shadows in the light of your potential. This transformation from fear to motivation is about mindset. When fear whispers, "You can't," respond with action—write a scene, develop a character, plot a twist. Every word written becomes a testament to your commitment, a step forward that turns fear into a drive to succeed.

Writing doesn't have to be a solitary endeavour. In fact, finding support within a community of fellow writers can be one of the most empowering steps you take. Writing groups and online forums are havens of encouragement, places where the shared experience of writing binds individuals together. Joining these communities provides not only feedback but also a sense of belonging. Others can offer fresh perspectives on your work, and their journeys may mirror your own. This camaraderie fosters a creative environment where ideas flourish and anxiety dissipates. Knowing that you're not alone and that others are navigating similar challenges can bolster your confidence and inspire you to keep pushing forward.

Embracing the writing process means acknowledging the fears that come with it and transforming them into strengths.

It's about crafting techniques to manage anxiety, turning fear into motivation, and seeking the support of a community that understands. Writing is a path filled with challenges but also with immense rewards. As you navigate this path, remember that each step forward is a triumph over fear, each page written a testament to your resolve. Embrace the creativity that flows from overcoming these obstacles. Let it guide you toward the story only you can tell.

Quill pens or laptops?

Some writers still use pen and paper – especially for first drafts. Others use old-fashioned word processors – as they say, it reduces the distractions of modern computers, especially in the internet age. Some writers have even written novels on their phones. Most, however, use a computer and software such as Microsoft Word (for planning many also use Microsoft Excel spreadsheets to help organize and structure chapters).

Microsoft Word – and today's Microsoft Office 360 – costs money, but there are free alternatives, for example Google Docs. This cloud-based software has many of the formatting options of Word and, because it's in the cloud, you're never in danger of losing your work.

Other (distraction-free) software specifically for writers has been created, and you may find you like one of them, for example: FocusWriter, WriteMonkey, CalmlyWriter or 750 Words.

My (sophisticated) 'weapon of choice' is Scrivener, which allows all aspects of a novel to be collected under one roof.

Get the right technology

From the quill to the spellcheck, technology has always played an important role for writers. Today digital technology is helping writers to research, plan, write, improve, share and store their stories. And remember – back it up, even by simply sending yourself an email copy of the Work in Progress!

CHAPTER 2

PLOT DEVELOPMENT MASTERY

Picture this: a reader tucked into their favourite armchair, eyes glued to the pages of your novel. They're so engrossed that the world around them fades away, and your story becomes their universe.

This magnetic pull is the magic of a well-crafted plot arc. It's the backbone of every unforgettable novel, holding the structure together while giving life to the narrative. Think of it as a rollercoaster designed to take your reader on a ride filled with anticipation, thrills, and that satisfying descent into resolution.

Plot arc

Crafting a compelling plot arc begins with understanding its core components, much like assembling the pieces of a puzzle to reveal a complete picture. We start with the exposition, where the scene is set and characters are introduced. This is where you lay the groundwork, offering readers a glimpse of the world they'll be inhabiting. Next comes the inciting incident, that pivotal moment that propels your protagonist into action. It's the catalyst that kicks the story into motion, creating a wave that carries everything forward. Think of it as the spark that lights the fuse, igniting the journey ahead.

Rising action

As the story progresses, we enter the rising action, where tension builds, and complexities multiply. This is the meat of your narrative, where characters are tested, stakes are raised, and the plot thickens. Every decision and conflict leads to the climactic turning point—a peak of intensity where the outcome hangs in the balance. It's the moment readers have been holding their breath for, the culmination of all that tension and anticipation. From there, we move into the falling action, where loose ends are tied up, and the dust begins to settle. Finally, the resolution offers closure, wrapping up the narrative and leaving your readers with a lingering sense of satisfaction or contemplation.

A character-driven plot is where the magic truly happens, intertwining plot progression with character development. Imagine your characters as the engine powering the story forward, their motivations and growth directly influencing the narrative's trajectory. This approach creates a dynamic interplay between character and plot, where each fuels the other. As characters evolve, so too does the plot, offering rich opportunities for emotional depth and resonance. By aligning character arcs with plot progression, you craft a narrative that feels organic and compelling, inviting readers to invest emotionally in both the journey and the outcome.

Surprise

The art of surprise lies in balancing predictability with innovation. While readers crave the comfort of familiar structures, they also yearn for the unexpected twists that keep them guessing. The challenge is to strike a balance between these two desires, crafting a narrative that feels both fresh and satisfying. Consider weaving in unexpected developments that still adhere to the internal logic of your story. These surprises should feel earned, not contrived, maintaining the delicate equilibrium between anticipation and revelation. A well-executed twist can breathe new life into your narrative, leaving readers delighted and eager for more.

Storyboards

Visualizing and organizing your plot can be immensely helpful, and this is where tools like plot outlines and storyboards come into play. They serve as roadmaps, guiding you through the intricacies of your narrative. Storyboarding techniques can help you visualize the flow of events, providing a bird's-eye view of your plot's structure. Crafting scene-by-scene outlines allows you to focus on the finer details, ensuring each moment serves a purpose and contributes to the overall arc. These tools are invaluable, offering clarity and coherence as you navigate the complexities of plot development.

GAINING INSPIRATION

Genre

Dive into the genre you want to write in—it's an exciting and essential step on your journey as an author! Immerse yourself in a variety of books to truly grasp their nuances. Think about the stories that inspire you—what books do you wish you'd written? Identify their genres and explore the masterpieces within.

Take notes on what resonates with you—the triumphs, the challenges, and everything in between. As you read, focus on the key elements of storytelling and style, paying attention to how they intertwine in each narrative.

Additionally, don't forget to check out online reviews to uncover what readers love about these books. This insight can be incredibly valuable in shaping your own writing style.

The more you explore your chosen genre, the clearer the connections among character, plot, and language will become. Embrace this research process; it's a fantastic way to refine your skills and develop your unique voice. With each book you read, you're not just learning—you're fuelling your passion for storytelling and steadily moving closer to crafting your own captivating novel

Go Wide

Read as much and as widely as possible and see how other writers construct their scenes, tease the reader, build tension.

Don't be afraid, especially when starting out, to steal or imitate – all art begins with imitation.

Compare notes

Make friends with writers who do not write like you. Swap books. Show each other work. Take the long view and the wide view.

Writing adds your lifetime to the lifetime of everyone else who has written or read, or who will read or write, including non-'literary' folk. All sorts of people work carefully or lovingly or effectively with words.

REFLECTION EXERCISE: CRAFT YOUR PLOT ARC

Take a moment to sketch out your plot arc. Identify your inciting incident, pinpoint the climactic turning point, and outline the resolution. Consider how your characters' motivations align with these events. Reflect on how you can balance predictability with surprise and use storyboarding techniques to visualize your narrative flow. This exercise will provide a solid foundation for crafting a plot that captivates and resonates with readers.

WEAVING SUBPLOTS SEAMLESSLY

The tapestry of the plot

Imagine your story as a tapestry, with the main plotline serving as the bold, central thread that holds everything together. Now picture the subplots as the intricate patterns woven throughout, adding richness and depth. Subplots are not just side stories; they are embellishments that make your narrative more vibrant and engaging. They allow you to explore themes and characters in a way the main plot might not permit. But to use them effectively, you need to differentiate them from the main plot and understand their unique role. While the main plot drives the core narrative, subplots enrich it by adding layers of complexity and intrigue.

Subplot interconnection

Creating subplots that interconnect smoothly with the main plot requires finesse. Think of them as tributaries feeding into a larger river, each contributing its unique flavour and impact. One technique involves creating thematic connections between your plots. If your main story explores themes of freedom, perhaps a subplot could delve into the cost of that freedom through a secondary character's journey. Such connections reinforce the central themes, creating a cohesive narrative experience. Subplots also offer the perfect stage to flesh out secondary characters. These characters can have their own arcs, motivations, and conflicts, providing readers with a more rounded view of your story's world. By doing so, you make your secondary characters feel as real and vital as your protagonist.

Beginnings, middle and ends

Subplots, like any good story, need a beginning, middle, and end. Each should have its own arc, a mini journey that feels complete and satisfying. Start by introducing a subplot with an event or issue that piques interest. Develop the subplot by introducing challenges or conflicts that test the characters involved. Finally, bring the subplot to a resolution that ties back to the main narrative, enriching the overall story. This structure ensures your subplots are not just filler but integral parts of the narrative tapestry. They should echo the main story's themes, offering new perspectives and insights, while standing strong on their own.

Juggle with coherence

Balancing subplots with the main narrative can feel like juggling, but it's crucial for maintaining coherence. Too many subplots, or ones that overshadow the main plot can confuse readers and dilute the story's impact. Regularly track each subplot's progression alongside the main plot to maintain balance. Ask yourself how each subplot contributes to the main story's development. If a subplot feels disconnected or distracts from the primary narrative, consider tightening its focus or integrating it more closely with the main events. This approach ensures that subplots enrich rather than overwhelm, enhancing the reader's experience without pulling focus from the central plot.

Style – text betrays the writer

Do not think that you should write something 'literary', to have to use all kinds of metaphors, complex syntax and philosophical musings to tell my story. Write the way you speak. Never start by thinking you have to write something complicated or deliberate, or because you think you have to develop your own sophisticated style, but simply because you want to tell a particular story or describe a specific scene. Your style will appear all by itself. It always does. All text betrays the writer.

Elevation through subplots

Maintaining this balance is about finesse and attention to detail. A subplot should feel like a natural extension of the main story, not an awkward appendage. Keep an eye on pacing—subplots should ebb and flow with the main narrative, providing respite or tension as needed. Use them to deepen character development, explore new themes, or introduce fresh conflicts. When done well, subplots can elevate your story, providing depth and texture that keeps readers engaged from the first page to the last.

MAINTAINING NARRATIVE TENSION

Imagine your story as a tightly wound string, vibrating with energy and anticipation. This is the essence of narrative tension, the invisible force that keeps readers gripped, flipping pages late into the night. But how do you create and sustain this tension throughout your narrative? The answer lies in carefully choosing and orchestrating the sources of tension. Begin by introducing conflicts that challenge your characters and raise the stakes. These conflicts can be external, like a looming threat or antagonist, or internal, such as a moral dilemma or personal fear. The key is to ensure these conflicts are significant enough to matter to your characters and, by extension, your readers. Introducing high stakes—where characters stand to lose or gain something valuable—fuels tension, making readers care about the outcome. Pacing techniques also play a crucial role. By varying the rhythm of your story, you can build suspense and create moments of high intensity. Quick, short sentences can convey urgency, while longer, more descriptive passages allow for reflection and anticipation.

Cliffhangers and foreshadowing are your allies in maintaining tension. Think of a cliffhanger as a door left tantalizingly ajar at the end of a chapter, inviting readers to peek through and wonder what's on the other side. Crafting effective chapter endings that leave questions unanswered or introduce a new twist can compel readers to keep going. Foreshadowing, on the other hand, is like planting seeds early in your narrative that blossom into significant plot points later. These subtle clues hint at future events, creating a sense of anticipation as readers piece together the puzzle. Done well, foreshadowing can deepen the reader's engagement, rewarding them for their attention to detail. The balance lies in being subtle enough to intrigue without giving too much away, maintaining a delicate dance between revelation and mystery.

Conflict

Establishing a clear central conflict is essential for anchoring your plot and providing focus to your narrative. If you're a first-time novelist or a new writer, consider looking to thrillers, fantasy, or adventure stories for examples of engaging 'good guy versus bad guy' conflicts. Conflict is beneficial because it clarifies motivations.

...And relief

While tension is vital, it's important to balance it with moments of relief. Imagine tension as a high note in music;

without the occasional rest, it can become overwhelming. These moments of relief allow readers to catch their breath, reflect, and process the narrative's events. They can be softer scenes that delve into character relationships, offer humour, or explore quieter aspects of the story. This ebb and flow of tension and relief helps maintain overall engagement, preventing reader fatigue and ensuring that the high points of your narrative stand out. These contrasting moments make the tension more impactful, much like the way a whisper can sound louder after a shout.

Revising to maximize tension is an iterative process. Once your draft is complete, revisit your manuscript with a critical eye. Look for areas where tension wanes or where opportunities for suspense are missed. Consider restructuring scenes to heighten conflict or revisiting character motivations to ensure stakes are clear and compelling. Pay attention to pacing, ensuring that the narrative's rhythm supports the tension you're building. This might mean cutting unnecessary scenes, tightening dialogue, or even expanding on moments that deserve more depth. The goal is to keep your readers on the edge of their seats, eager to see how the story unfolds. Editing with tension in mind ensures that every chapter, scene, and sentence serves the overarching goal of engaging and thrilling your audience, creating a narrative that resonates long after the final page is turned.

STRUCTURE YOUR NOVEL

Once you have a clear idea of your story concept, you will need to define an essential aspect of how you're going to tell it. This is the story's structure – what happens when. While this may seem simple if not obvious, the structure must be carefully considered to ensure that the story makes sense as well as compelling the reader to read on. There is no specific 'best structure', but there are devices and methods to guide yours.

At the highest level, most stories have a beginning, a middle and an end. This has been translated into the three-act structure, already referenced in this guide.

- ACT 1: Inciting incident
- ACT 2: The journey, rising action, challenges
- ACT 3: Resolution

Consider the following devices that can be used within the wider structure to compel readers throughout and deliver a satisfying end.

- What is the setting? Where are we, what's going on and to whom?
- The promise. Suggesting what the story will deliver if the reader reads on
- The trigger/inciting incident. Something happens or changes and something needs to be done about it
- The quest. What must be done?
- Raising the stakes. Make the quest more important, weigh it down with potential repercussions
- Heighten the drama with surprises and twists by subverting their expectations
- Critical choice. The protagonist commits to doing something
- The quest reaches its peak; the culmination of the action

- Things finally start to go the protagonist's way for once (though you might choose to subvert this and have things get even worse)
- The results of the climax and reversal; delivering the promise.

While you don't have to stick to this structure, you might want to see how your story idea maps onto this, and what might be happening in your story to deliver these.

Other structural story elements that you can use, include:

- Refusal of the call
- Meeting the mentor
- Crossing the threshold
- Tests and trials
- Approach the innermost cave/sanctum/lair
- The ordeal
- Reward
- Road back
- Resurrection

We described Planners and Pantsers earlier – it is important as a novel develops that there is a sense of where it will lead. Sometimes it is the characters that decide!

PLOTTING WITH PURPOSE: THEMES AND SYMBOLS

Themes are the heartbeat of a story, the underlying currents that give your narrative depth and resonance. Identifying your core themes early in the writing process can guide the decisions you make about plot, character, and setting. It's not about forcing a message onto your readers, but rather about allowing these themes to naturally emerge through your story. Perhaps you're writing about the complexity of love, the struggle for identity, or the pursuit of freedom. Whatever the theme, it's important to weave it into the fabric of your narrative subtly, letting it inform the characters' actions and the plot's development without overshadowing the story itself.

Symbols, on the other hand, are like secret codes embedded within your narrative, adding layers and depth to the storytelling. They can be powerful tools for conveying themes, creating a richer reading experience. A recurring motif, such as a lone tree standing against the storm, might symbolize resilience or isolation. The key is to choose symbols that resonate with the themes you're exploring and to use them sparingly enough that they enrich rather than clutter the narrative. Symbols should emerge organically, not as contrived elements inserted for effect. They can be objects, colours, or even actions that carry deeper meanings, adding an extra dimension to your story.

Aligning themes with character arcs ensures that the themes are not just abstract ideas but are grounded in the characters' journeys. As your characters develop and change, their experiences should reflect and reinforce the themes. If your theme is redemption, for instance, your protagonist's arc might follow their struggle to overcome past mistakes and seek forgiveness. This alignment creates a narrative where the themes and characters are in harmony, each enhancing the other. The themes should feel like an integral part of the characters' lives, shaping their decisions and growth as the plot unfolds.

Subtlety is crucial when integrating themes and symbols. Heavy-handedness can turn readers off, making the story feel preachy or didactic. Instead, employ the "show, don't tell" technique to let themes and symbols speak for themselves. Let your characters' actions and dialogues reveal the themes, allowing readers to uncover the layers themselves. A character's quiet moment of reflection, their choice in a critical situation, or a seemingly mundane object that holds significant meaning can all convey themes without overt explanation. This subtlety invites readers to engage with the story on a deeper level, drawing their own connections and interpretations.

As you plot with purpose, remember that themes and symbols are tools to enhance your storytelling, not constraints to limit it. They add richness and texture, inviting readers to explore the nuances of your narrative. By embedding these elements thoughtfully and subtly, you create a story that resonates not just in the moment but lingers in the minds and hearts of your readers long after they've turned the last page.

AVOIDING COMMON PLOT PITFALLS

In the midst of things

By focusing on action and activity, you will grip your readers more than if you have pages and pages of back story, scene setting, description or world-building. All of this may be important, and you'll get to it, but it's more important to grip your reader *first.* And by making them feel like they're in the middle of something, they are more likely to be gripped. Back-filling the setting can add interest for the reader, who is piecing things together.

Cliches

Steering clear of plot clichés is like dodging potholes on a scenic drive. They sneak up on you, and if you're not careful, they can jolt your readers out of an otherwise engaging story. Clichés are those well-trodden paths that lead to predictability, and nobody wants a story that feels like a rerun. Recognizing them is the first step. Think of the damsel in distress or the wise mentor who dies just before the final battle. These tropes have been done to death, and while they might have their place, relying on them as the backbone of your plot can sap originality. Instead, aim to twist these clichés. Give your mentor a mysterious past, or let that damsel save herself. The goal is to take familiar elements and flip them on their heads, surprising your readers while keeping them hooked.

Plot Logic

Maintaining plot logic and consistency is crucial. Your story world should operate under its own set of rules, much like a well-oiled machine. These rules establish the boundaries within which your characters operate, ensuring that events unfold in a believable way. If your world has magic, for instance, outline its limits. Can everyone use magic, or is it restricted? What are its costs? Establishing clear rules not only enhances believability but also prevents plot holes—those pesky gaps that leave readers scratching their heads. By maintaining consistency, you build trust with your audience, allowing them to fully immerse themselves in the world you've created.

Plot holes and unresolved threads can unravel even the most intricate narratives. They're like loose threads on a sweater—left unchecked, they can ruin the whole piece. Thorough plotting is your best defence against these pitfalls. Create a timeline of events and track character arcs to ensure everything aligns. If your protagonist discovers a secret in chapter three, make sure it's addressed by the end. Unresolved threads can leave readers feeling unsatisfied. They deserve a complete picture, where every subplot and detail ties back to the main narrative. Consider keeping a checklist of plot points and resolutions. This way, you can systematically ensure that every question posed is eventually answered, leaving no stone unturned.

The Alchemical Relationship

Exploring the relationship between story ideas, structure, and plot is a fascinating journey—one that combines elements of science and a touch of artful magic!

Plot: This encompasses the series of events that shape your narrative, detailing not only what happens but also the intricate connections between those events and their timing.

Structure: This represents the blueprint of your story, the framework that holds everything together.

While we discuss plot after structure here, it's important to remember that this isn't a strict hierarchy. The writing process is wonderfully fluid, and you have the freedom to tweak either element as your story evolves. For instance, the overarching plot might remain constant, but you might shuffle the order in which details are revealed to create suspense or surprise. Once you have crafted your story's structure, it's time to dive into the specifics of your plot.

Using tools like tables or spreadsheets can be incredibly beneficial for organizing your plot and structure.

Consider creating columns for 'conflict', 'purpose', and 'motivation' to ensure every segment has a clear direction and purpose. Many new writers find this approach invaluable, as it helps maintain the pace of the story telling.

Complexity

Complexity in storytelling is a double-edged sword. While it can enrich your narrative, too much can lead to confusion. The trick is to balance complexity with clarity, making sure your plot remains understandable. Simplifying convoluted plot points doesn't mean dumbing down your story. Instead, it involves distilling the essence of each scene and character, ensuring clarity without sacrificing depth. If a scene doesn't serve the plot, consider cutting it or combining it with another. Each element should be a cog in the larger machine, working in tandem to propel the story forward. A plot should be like a well-choreographed dance, where every move has purpose, and no step is wasted.

As we wrap up this chapter on plot development, remember that a well-crafted plot is more than just a series of events. It's an intricate tapestry of ideas, characters, and emotions, woven together with care and intention. By avoiding clichés, ensuring consistency, and balancing complexity, you create a narrative that captivates and resonates. This foundation sets the stage for the next chapter, where we'll explore the art of character creation and how these figures breathe life into the plots you've crafted.

CHAPTER 3
CHARACTER CREATION AND DEVELOPMENT

CHOOSING YOUR NOVEL'S POINT OF VIEW

The choice of perspective in your storytelling is truly pivotal; it shapes how readers experience your novel. Here are the primary points of view to consider: -

- **First Person:** This intimate style allows the narrator, who is also the protagonist, to share their journey directly with "I."
- **Second Person:** A unique and less common perspective that can offer a fresh, engaging experience, though you'll require careful crafting. If you know what I mean -it's like I'm telling you how to behave. You should read Jay McInerney's Bright Lights, Big City to get the idea.
- **Third Person:** Here, an unseen narrator unfolds the narrative, granting a broader view of the characters and their interactions.

To help you select the perfect point of view, reflect on these guiding questions:

- What level of connection or distance do you wish to create between the reader and the narrator?
- How much insight and information should the reader gather from the story?
- How important is the narrator's reliability to your plot?
- Would multiple perspectives enhance the richness of your narrative? The Art of Character Creation and Development

Imagine opening a book and instantly meeting a character so vivid that they feel alive. You can visualize their hopes, fears, and struggles, experiencing their journey as if it were your own. This enchanting bond arises from well-developed characters. In this section, we'll dive into the fascinating process of creating and nurturing unforgettable characters. They are not merely names on a page; they breathe life into your story and draw readers in. Crafting them with depth and nuance is essential for capturing your audience's heart and keeping them

BUILDING COMPLEX CHARACTER PROFILES

Character foundations

Let's begin by establishing the foundational details of your characters. Think of this as sketching the outlines before filling in the colours. Start by deciding on the basics: name, age, background, and physical traits. What does your character look like? Do they have a signature style or a distinguishing feature, like a scar or a peculiar twinkle in their eye? Consider their background—were they raised in a bustling city or a quiet village? These details form the canvas upon which their personality is painted. Creating detailed character sheets can be immensely helpful. They serve as a reference point, ensuring consistency as your characters evolve throughout the story. List their quirks and habits, those little nuances that make them unique. Maybe your character always carries a pocket watch, or perhaps they have a habit of tapping their foot when anxious. These small touches add depth and relatability, transforming them from mere words into vivid personas.

Character intricacies

Beyond the basics, delve into the intricacies of their personalities. Characters, like real people, are a tapestry of strengths and weaknesses. Identify their unique talents—perhaps your protagonist is a skilled musician, or maybe they possess an uncanny knack for solving puzzles. But remember, flaws are just as important. A character who is too perfect can feel flat and unrelatable. Balance their virtues with vices; maybe your character is brave but reckless or kind yet naive. These contrasts create dynamic personalities that engage readers. Exploring both sides of your characters invites readers into a richer, more nuanced narrative, where characters are as unpredictable as they are intriguing.

Internal landscapes

Characters are not just defined by their external traits; their internal landscapes are equally vital. This is where you explore their thoughts, fears, and aspirations. What keeps your character up at night? What dreams do they chase, and what nightmares haunt them? Mapping out internal conflicts can add layers to your character development. Perhaps they struggle with self-doubt despite outward confidence, or maybe they wrestle with loyalty to family versus personal ambition. Developing comprehensive backstories can further illuminate these inner worlds. Consider their past—how did their childhood shape their present? Did a pivotal event set them on the path they now walk? By understanding where your characters come from, you can better predict how they might respond to the challenges you throw their way.

Relationships

Relationships and dynamics are the spice that flavours your characters' lives. No character exists in a vacuum; their interactions with others shape their growth and drive the plot. Think about the people surrounding your character. Design family trees and social networks to visualize these connections. How do these relationships influence your character's decisions and development? Perhaps a sibling rivalry fuels their competitive nature, or a mentor's guidance steers them toward their destiny. Exploring power dynamics between characters can also add complexity to your narrative. Who holds the influence in their relationships, and how does this shift over time? These interactions can drive conflict, reveal hidden depths, and propel the story forward.

CHARACTER DEVELOPMENT EXERCISE: CRAFTING PROFILES

Take a moment to craft a detailed profile for one of your main characters. Start with the basics—name, age, and physical description. Then, delve into their personality, identifying both strengths and weaknesses. Explore their internal landscape, noting key fears, desires, and conflicts. Finally, map out their relationships and how these dynamics influence their development. Use this profile as a living document, updating it as your character evolves throughout the story. This exercise will serve as a valuable tool, guiding your character creation process and ensuring consistency and depth in your narrative.

Character planning Notes

Use this as a template to help describe key characters

Character Name
Age
Location
Role in Story
Goal
Physical Description
Personality
Occupation
Habits / Mannerisms
Background
Internal Conflicts
External Conflicts
Notes

DEVELOPING AUTHENTIC CHARACTER ARCS

Character journeys

Crafting a character arc is like plotting a journey. You start with an idea, a sense of where you want to go, and then you map out the path to get there. Begin by defining your character's starting point. This is where they stand when your story opens—their worldview, their ambitions, their flaws. Imagine your character as they are at the beginning, a snapshot of their life before everything changes. Are they content in their routine, or restless for something more? Are they an outsider looking in, or the life of the party? This "before" snapshot lays the groundwork for their transformation. It's the baseline against which all changes will be measured, the calm before the storm.

Character transformation

As your story unfolds, so too does your character's transformation. This isn't about flipping a switch and changing overnight; it's about the slow, gradual evolution that happens as they face challenges and grow. Identify the pivotal moments, those catalysts that spark change in your character. Perhaps it's a life-altering decision, a chance encounter, or an unexpected loss. These moments are the heartbeat of your character's transformation, pushing them to question their beliefs and confront their fears. Plan these changes thoughtfully, allowing room for realizations and growth. A character arc is often a series of small shifts leading to a significant change. It's about progress, not perfection.

Character growth

Your character's growth should mirror the plot's progression, each step forward in their arc aligned with key events in the story. When your plot moves, your character should move too. A plot twist might challenge their morality, forcing them to reevaluate their values. A climax might demand courage they didn't know they had. By correlating character growth with plot milestones, you weave a narrative where both elements enhance each other. It's a dance between character and plot, each influencing the other, creating a seamless, cohesive story. This integration ensures your characters feel like they belong in their world, their development a natural response to the events unfolding around them.

The conclusion of a character arc is a delicate balance. It's about crafting an ending that not only ties up loose ends but also reflects the internal journey your character has undergone. What have they learned? How have they changed? The resolution should feel satisfying, a culmination of the transformation they've experienced. Perhaps they've found clarity in a world of chaos, or maybe they've learned to embrace their flaws and strengths alike. The key is to ensure that the conclusion resonates with the journey. It should feel earned, not forced, a natural extension of the narrative. This resolution is the final brushstroke on the canvas of your character's life, bringing everything into focus.

In developing authentic character arcs, remember that change is at the core. It's about taking your characters from one state to another, crafting a narrative that captures the essence of growth and transformation. It's about the journey they take, the challenges they face, and the person they become. Through these arcs, you invite readers to walk alongside your characters, witnessing their struggles and triumphs, and perhaps even seeing a bit of themselves in the stories you tell.

CRAFTING DISTINCTIVE DIALOGUE

Character voices

When you think of your favourite characters, often it's their voices that stand out. Their words echo in your mind long after you've closed the book. Capturing those unique character voices is crucial for any aspiring writer. Imagine a character from the bustling streets of New York. Their speech might be peppered with sharp, quick phrases, reflecting the city's fast pace. Contrast that with someone from the deep South, where the drawl might stretch words into long, lyrical sentences. Using dialects and slang appropriately can paint vivid pictures of your characters' backgrounds and personalities. But remember, it's a delicate dance. Overuse can turn vibrant dialogue into a caricature, so sprinkle these elements like seasoning—just enough to enhance, but not overpower.

Dialogue to advance the story

Dialogue is more than mere conversation; it's a tool to advance the plot and reveal the soul of your characters. Imagine a tense dinner scene where every polite word exchanged is layered with unspoken tension. Here, subtext becomes your ally, weaving in what's left unsaid. Maybe a character's seemingly innocent question is a veiled challenge, or a simple "I'm fine" hides a storm of emotions. Crafting dialogue-driven conflict isn't about shouting matches; it's about the subtle power plays, the words chosen as weapons. Through these exchanges, characters reveal their true selves, their fears, their desires. Dialogue can be the heartbeat of a scene, driving the narrative forward with every beat.

Natural dialogue

Natural and engaging dialogue can make or break a story. The aim is to write conversations that sound real yet are more than just small talk. Imagine overhearing a conversation at a café; it flows, it pauses, it picks up again. But in writing, every word must serve a purpose. Stilted or forced dialogue sticks out like a sore thumb, breaking the reader's immersion. Dialogue must balance with action and description to maintain rhythm. A character might gesture wildly while speaking or pause to watch the rain trickle down a window. These actions ground the dialogue, making it feel lived-in and dynamic. Think of dialogue as a dance partner to action, each moving in harmony to keep the reader engaged.

Conversations do more than just fill pages; they build and deepen relationships between characters. Imagine two friends bantering over a cup of coffee, their playful repartee revealing years of shared history and affection. Banter is more than witty exchanges; it's the shorthand of friendship, the language of closeness. It can also reflect power shifts. A seemingly simple conversation can reveal who holds influence, who's challenging authority, or who's seeking approval. Through dialogue, characters negotiate their relationships, test boundaries, and forge connections. These moments are where characters truly come alive, where their interactions breathe life into the story, and where relationships evolve and deepen naturally.

DIALOGUE EXERCISE: VOICE EXPLORATION

Take a scene from your story and rewrite it from each character's perspective. Focus on how their backgrounds and personalities influence their speech. Does one character speak in clipped sentences while another rambles? Use this exercise to refine each character's voice, ensuring it remains distinct and true to who they are. This will help you understand your characters better and create dialogue that resonates authentically with readers.

EXPLORING DIVERSE CHARACTER MOTIVATIONS

Character Motivations

Understanding what motivates your characters is like unlocking the secret sauce to their actions and decisions. Imagine your character standing at a crossroads. Why do they choose one path over another? This is where their core motivations and desires come into play. These are the inner forces that propel them through your story. Begin by identifying both primary and secondary motivations. The primary motivation might be something grand, like seeking justice for a wrong, while secondary motivations could be personal, such as yearning for acceptance or battling a fear of failure. These layers create depth, making characters feel real and relatable. Aligning these motivations with their backstories adds coherence. Perhaps a character's drive for justice stems from witnessing an injustice in their past. This connection between their history and their current desires makes motivations feel authentic and organic.

External and internal motivators

As you delve deeper, it's crucial to distinguish between external and internal motivators. External motivators are the outside forces that push your character forward. Think of these as the circumstances or pressures that demand action—like a looming deadline or a rival's challenge. Internal motivators, on the other hand, are the desires and fears rooted in your character's psyche. Maybe they're driven by a need for recognition or haunted by a fear of being forgotten. By examining both, you gain insight into your character's behaviour. These motivators often work in tandem, influencing decisions in complex ways. A character might pursue a promotion (external) because they seek validation from a parent (internal). Understanding this dynamic helps you craft characters whose actions resonate as true and compelling.

Conflicts

Conflicts often arise when motivations clash, either within the character or between characters. These conflicts are the lifeblood of your narrative, driving the plot forward. Picture a character torn between loyalty to a friend and ambition for a coveted position. This internal struggle can create tension, leading to decisions that define their arc. Similarly, clashing motivations between characters—like two siblings vying for their parents' approval—can spark external conflicts that propel the story. The key is to ensure these motivations are believable and understandable to the reader. They should stem from the character's established traits and history, not feel like conveniences to serve the plot. When motivations are well-crafted, conflicts flow naturally, providing the narrative with a rich tapestry of tension and resolution.

As your characters evolve, so too should their motivations. Just as people change over time, so do their desires and drives. This evolution reflects their growth and the impact of their experiences. Perhaps a character starts out seeking revenge but, through the story's events, learns the value of forgiveness. These shifts should feel natural, a culmination of the journey they've undertaken. Reflecting this growth through altered desires adds authenticity and complexity. It's about showing how the character's perspective has shifted, how their priorities have realigned. These changes can be subtle or profound, but they should always feel earned, a result of the character's interactions and choices. By allowing motivations to evolve, you create a dynamic narrative that mirrors the fluid nature of real life, keeping readers invested in your characters' journeys.

Elevate the Stakes!

What truly matters in your novel? Is it the future of our planet, the journey of a cherished relationship, or the pursuit of dreams?

Let's define those stakes clearly:

- What does your character risk losing?
- What incredible rewards are within their reach?
- What steps must they take to secure their gains and avoid loss?
- What challenges lurk in their path?
- What are they willing to risk in their quest for success?

No matter how high the stakes currently are, consider boosting them or adding new dimensions to the scenario! This not only captivates your readers but also intensifies their investment in the journey, leading to more profound relief and satisfaction when resolution comes.

As you craft your story, keep the stakes escalating, ensuring that:

- The losses become more significant
- The rewards grow more enticing
- Their tasks are more demanding
- New, unexpected obstacles emerge

This approach will deepen the tension and excitement, making your narrative truly unforgettable!

The situation is hopeless

To enhance excitement and create a satisfying resolution, it's effective to portray the situation as seemingly hopeless. How does the protagonist ultimately overcome this challenge? Introduce fresh, unexpected obstacles that initially stand in their way, only to be removed later. It's fascinating to see how many narratives guide us down one solution, only to divert us before unveiling an overlooked element that leads to success. This twist not only heightens tension but also makes the resolution even more rewarding. Let's get ready for a thrilling journey of perseverance and discovery!

TECHNIQUES FOR CHARACTER GROWTH

Imagine your character standing at a crossroads, facing challenges that test their limits. These challenges are the catalysts for growth, pushing them beyond their comfort zones. Both external and internal conflicts play a role here. Externally, they might face obstacles like a formidable antagonist or a seemingly insurmountable quest. Internally, they could be wrestling with self-doubt or moral dilemmas. These trials are not just plot devices; they're transformative moments that shape your character's evolution. Think about designing trials that are specific to your character's weaknesses, forcing them to confront and overcome them. This struggle is what makes them relatable, as readers see parts of themselves in these battles.

Growth in a character is often illustrated through their actions and decisions. It's those pivotal moments where they choose to act differently that highlight their development. Maybe your character decides to forgive instead of holding a grudge, or they finally stand up to a bully. These choices should feel significant, reflecting a shift in their perspective. As a writer, you have the opportunity to show this change through meaningful actions that speak louder than words. Highlight these decision-making moments and let them serve as milestones in your character's journey. This approach not only drives the narrative forward but also deepens the reader's investment in your character's story.

Reflecting on a character's past can provide valuable insights into their growth. Consider how their history influences their current responses to challenges. Flashbacks can be a useful tool here, offering glimpses of key formative events that have left a mark. Perhaps a childhood incident taught them to distrust others, or a past betrayal made them wary of new relationships. By weaving these elements into your story, you offer readers a richer understanding of your character's motivations. These reflections are not just about explaining behaviour; they're about showing how past experiences inform present choices. As your character faces new trials, their history should guide their transformation, adding layers to their development.

Balancing growth with consistency is crucial to maintaining character integrity. As your characters evolve, they should remain true to their core essence. Growth doesn't mean abandoning who they are; it's about becoming a fuller version of themselves. For instance, a character who's inherently kind might become more assertive without losing their compassion. Ensure that changes in your character feel natural and believable, not forced or out of character. This balance is key to crafting characters that resonate with readers, as they see growth that feels genuine and earned. Remember, growth is a process, not a complete overhaul. It's about subtle shifts that align with the character's established traits, creating a coherent and satisfying arc.

As we wrap up this chapter on character growth, remember that your characters are the heart of your story. Their development is what keeps readers engaged, rooting for them through every twist and turn. By introducing challenges, illustrating growth through choices, reflecting on past influences, and balancing change with consistency, you create characters that feel real and dynamic. Characters who grow and change enrich your narrative, inviting readers to invest emotionally in their stories. Next, we'll explore how the worlds these characters inhabit can be just as compelling, shaping their journeys and adding depth to your storytelling.

CHAPTER 4
SETTING AND WORLDBUILDING

Picture this: a reader diving into your novel and finding themselves in a bustling marketplace where spices linger in the air, a cacophony of voices echo around them, and vibrant fabrics dance in the wind. The scene is so vivid that they can almost smell the cinnamon and feel the sun on their face. That's the power of a well-crafted setting. It's the silent character in your story, providing context and depth, shaping your characters, and influencing your plot. It transports readers to new worlds, making your narrative come alive in their imagination.

DESIGNING VIVID LANDSCAPES

Tapping the senses

Creating environments that leap off the page involves tapping into the senses. When you describe a setting, think about what your characters see, hear, smell, taste, and touch. This is sensory language at work, and it's magic for bringing your writing to life. Imagine your character stepping into a forest. Instead of simply stating that it's a forest, paint a picture with words. Describe the towering trees, their leaves whispering secrets in the breeze. Let the reader hear the crunch of twigs underfoot, smell the damp earth after a fresh rain, and feel the cool air that carries the scent of pine. Specificity is your friend here. The more specific your descriptions, the more vivid the picture you create.

Evoke mood and tone

To evoke mood and tone, your landscapes should reflect the emotions of your characters and the narrative. Imagine a scene where a character is feeling isolated. A barren, windswept plain might serve as the perfect backdrop, mirroring their loneliness. Conversely, a warm, bustling tavern can convey a sense of camaraderie. You can enhance the narrative's emotional impact by aligning the setting with your characters' emotions without spelling it out. This is an artful way to "show, don't tell," allowing readers to feel the story's mood organically.

Settings

Settings should do more than just look pretty; they should serve the story. Each element of the landscape should have a purpose, whether it's contributing to the plot or deepening character development. Consider a tale set in a coastal town where the tides play a crucial role in the story. The ebb and flow of the sea could symbolize change, reflecting the protagonist's inner turmoil. Or maybe the town square is where secrets are whispered, and alliances formed, becoming a hub of intrigue that drives the narrative forward. Purposeful inclusion of environmental features ensures that every detail adds to the story's richness, creating a cohesive and compelling world.

Creating landmarks

Developing unique geographical features can make your story stand out. These are the landmarks that readers will remember long after they've put the book down. Think of a mountain range shaped like a sleeping giant or a city built within the hollow of an ancient tree. These distinct locations not only add flair but also offer opportunities for creativity in plot and character interaction. Incorporating cultural or historical significance into these features can further enrich your world. Perhaps the mountain range is a sacred site, revered by the locals and central to the story's conflict. Or the city in the tree could house ancient secrets that propel the plot and challenge the characters.

REFLECTION EXERCISE: SENSORY EXPLORATION

Sensory language

Take a moment to close your eyes and imagine a setting from your story. What do you see? Hear? Smell? As you explore each sense, jot down vivid details that come to mind. Use these notes to craft a scene rich with sensory language, ensuring each detail serves the story. Consider how the setting reflects the narrative's mood and contributes to character development. This exercise will help you create immersive environments that captivate and engage your readers.

The canvas for your characters

By weaving sensory details into your settings, you create landscapes that are not just backdrops but integral parts of your story. These vivid environments invite readers to step into your world, experiencing it with all their senses. As you continue to build your narrative, let these settings serve as a canvas on which your characters' stories unfold, enhancing the depth and richness of your tale.

INTEGRATING SETTING WITH STORY

Weave the setting and the narrative

Think of setting as the silent partner in your narrative, always there, subtly shaping the reader's experience without demanding attention. To truly integrate setting with your story, it needs to be woven seamlessly into the narrative fabric rather than standing alone as mere description. Imagine a bustling city street during a chase scene. Instead of pausing to describe every detail, let the clatter of footsteps echo off the cobblestones as your characters sprint through narrow alleys, the smell of food vendors' carts wafting through the air with each sharp turn. The setting becomes a backdrop for action, enhancing the urgency and tension without halting the story's momentum.

Stormy weather

Just a small comment, but it was always a NaNoWriMo (National Novel Writers' Month) trick to be able to reach the 1,666 words per day wordcount by describing the weather. Use selectively.

Make the pivotal scenes pop

Aligning your settings with plot events can amplify key moments in your story, creating contrasts that make pivotal scenes pop. Picture a serene, sunlit garden where two characters share a tense, argumentative exchange. The tranquillity of the setting starkly contrasts with the emotional turmoil between them, heightening the impact of their conflict. Alternatively, a dark, stormy night might mirror a character's inner chaos as they face a moral dilemma. These contrasts can be powerful storytelling tools, underscoring the emotional stakes and drawing readers deeper into the narrative.

Reflection and contrast

By choosing settings that reflect or contrast with plot events, you add layers to the storytelling, creating a dynamic interplay between environment and action.

The setting isn't just about the physical space; it's also a lens through which we see characters. How your characters interact with their surroundings can reveal deep insights into their personalities and motivations. A character who pauses to admire a sunset might be introspective, seeking solace in nature, while another who rushes past without a glance could be consumed by their own concerns. Observing these interactions allows readers to glean understanding without explicit exposition. Settings can also influence character choices; a character might choose a familiar path through a forest because it reminds them of safer times or avoid a certain street corner due to past trauma. These decisions, informed by setting, add authenticity and depth to character development, making them feel real and relatable.

Underscore motifs of the story

Enhancing thematic elements through setting involves using the environment to underscore the themes and motifs of your story. Natural elements or locations can carry symbolic weight, adding resonance to your narrative. A river might symbolize the flow of time or the inevitability of change, while a mountain could represent an insurmountable challenge or personal growth. By embedding these symbols subtly into your settings, you reinforce the themes without overtly stating them. This symbolic use of setting invites readers to engage with the story on a deeper level, drawing connections and finding meaning beyond the surface. It transforms the setting into an active participant in the narrative, contributing to the richness and complexity of the story.

Depth and dimension

As you weave settings into your story, remember they are more than just the backdrop. They are vital threads in the tapestry of your narrative, influencing plot, revealing character, and enhancing themes. The setting should feel organic, a natural extension of the story that adds depth and dimension without overpowering the narrative. When done well, the setting becomes an immersive experience for the reader, drawing them into the world you've created and making the story feel alive and vibrant.

WORLDBUILDING: BEYOND THE BASICS

Societal structure and political nuance

Imagine creating a world where every societal structure and political nuance breathes life into your narrative. It's about diving deep into the way your society functions, from who leads to how power is distributed. Are there monarchies, democracies, or perhaps an oligarchy led by the wealthiest citizens? These systems of governance shape how characters interact with each other and the world around them. Picture a council of elders ruling a village, their wisdom revered, yet their decisions stirring tension among the younger generations eager for change. By crafting hierarchies that reflect power dynamics, you lend authenticity and complexity to your world.

Culture, power dynamics and historical context

Beyond the political, the cultural and historical layers of your world add richness and texture. Think about the festivals that bring communities together or the rituals that mark important life events. These cultural elements can serve as pivotal plot points or simply add depth to your setting. For instance, a harvest festival might be the backdrop for a crucial revelation or a time when tensions boil over. Consider also the historical events that have shaped your world. Perhaps a long-forgotten war still casts a shadow over the present, influencing politics and personal grudges. Establishing a timeline of key events can provide context and motivation for your characters' actions, making your world feel lived-in and real.

A believable ecosystem

A believable ecosystem is another cornerstone of your fictional world. It's not just about having trees and rivers, but about developing flora and fauna that fit seamlessly into the environment. Imagine a forest where luminescent plants glow at night, providing both beauty and a navigational aid for travellers. Or consider a desert with creatures that have adapted to its harsh climate, their survival skills becoming metaphorical lessons for your characters. Inventing unique species or ecological systems enriches your world, offering new challenges and opportunities for your plot. By considering how these ecosystems interact with your characters and their society, you create a world that feels coherent and interconnected.

Technology and magic?

Technology and magic are elements that can dramatically alter the landscape of your story, influencing everything from daily life to the balance of power. In a technologically advanced society, consider how innovations shape social structures and personal relationships. Perhaps a new invention disrupts the status quo, leading to conflict and change. Similarly, if magic is part of your world, it should have clear rules and limitations. What can it achieve, and what are its costs? Maybe magic is accessible to only a select few, creating a class divide that fuels tension. Crafting these rules ensures consistency and believability, allowing your readers to immerse themselves in the story without stumbling over inconsistencies.

Interplay between elements

The interplay between these elements—social structures, cultural traditions, ecosystems, and technological or magical influences—creates a rich tapestry that can elevate your narrative. It's about considering how each piece fits into the larger puzzle, affecting characters and plot in meaningful ways. These layers invite readers to explore your world, uncovering its secrets and understanding its intricacies. Whether you're crafting a sprawling fantasy realm or a small, intimate setting, these foundational elements provide the structure and depth needed to captivate and engage.

BALANCING REALISM AND IMAGINATION

Believability

Picture this: you're crafting a world where dragons soar above bustling cities, yet the laws of physics still hold sway. This blend of the familiar and the fantastical is what makes a story captivating. By combining real-world physics with fantastical phenomena, you ground your readers in a world that feels both magical and believable. Think of it like adding a pinch of fantasy into the everyday. Perhaps your characters live in a city where gravity is slightly altered, making everything feel just a little lighter, a little more magical. But the buildings still stand, people still walk, and life carries on with a hint of wonder. This balance keeps your audience intrigued, allowing them to suspend disbelief while staying anchored in reality. It's about maintaining a delicate equilibrium where the extraordinary coexists with the ordinary, inviting readers to explore the unknown with a sense of familiarity.

Internal consistency

To keep your world believable, internal consistency is crucial. Once you establish the rules of your universe, stick to them. If magic is a rare and exhausting talent, don't suddenly let every character wield it effortlessly in a climactic battle. This kind of inconsistency can break the reader's immersion, pulling them out of the story. Instead, think of your world-specific laws as the framework that holds your narrative together. They are the invisible threads that ensure everything makes sense within the context of your creation. When these rules are clear and consistent, they allow readers to fully invest in the world you've built, trusting in its logic and integrity.

Authenticity as a touchstone

Drawing inspiration from real-world cultures, places, or events can add authenticity to your fantastical settings. It's like giving your world a touchstone to reality. For instance, you might research ancient Rome to create a society that values honour and thrives on political intrigue. Or you could take inspiration from the serene landscapes of Kyoto to design a city that blends nature with architecture in harmony. By adapting historical events or locations, you create a rich tapestry that feels both new and familiar. This approach not only grounds your world in reality but also offers layers of depth and nuance. It challenges readers to find echoes of the real world in your narrative, enhancing the sense of wonder and connection.

Creative risks

Encouraging creative risks is where innovation truly thrives. Don't be afraid to push the boundaries of conventional storytelling. Maybe your world defies gravity entirely, with floating islands populated by nomadic tribes. Or perhaps you explore societal norms that challenge our understanding of community and individuality. These risks can open doors to unique narratives and fresh perspectives. They invite readers to step into the unexpected, to question what they know, and to embrace the unfamiliar. When you take these risks, you breathe new life into your world, crafting stories that linger in the minds of your readers long after they've turned the last page.

Balance between real and imagined

As you weave these elements together, remember that the heart of worldbuilding lies in the balance between the real and the imagined. It's about blending the known with the unknown, creating a tapestry of wonder and reality. This balance invites readers to explore the depths of your world, offering them a place where their imaginations can roam free while their feet remain firmly planted on familiar ground. By grounding your fantastical elements in realism, you create a narrative that is both enchanting and compelling, a world that feels as vivid and alive as our own.

In this chapter, you've learned how to craft settings that captivate and engage, blending realism with imagination to create worlds that are both believable and enchanting. As we move forward, we'll delve into the heart of dialogue, exploring how conversations can reveal character and drive plot. Dialogue is the lifeblood of storytelling, where characters come alive and stories unfold through their voices. Let's explore how to capture these voices with authenticity and flair.

CHAPTER 5
FINDING YOUR UNIQUE VOICE

Literary fingerprint

Imagine your writing style as your literary fingerprint—distinctive and unmistakably yours. It's what sets your stories apart, making readers recognize your work with just a few lines. Finding this unique style is a journey of exploration and discovery, where you uncover the elements that resonate with your inner storyteller. Your voice is more than just the words you choose; it's the rhythm and cadence of your sentences, the perspective you bring, and the emotions you evoke. This chapter is all about finding and refining that voice, turning it into a signature style that feels as comfortable as your favourite sweater.

DISCOVERING YOUR WRITING STYLE

Immersion in styles and genres

The first step in discovering your writing style is to immerse yourself in diverse writing styles and genres. Think of it as a literary buffet, where you sample everything from classic literature to contemporary fiction, and even those quirky experimental works that defy categorization. Each genre offers a unique perspective on storytelling, giving you insights into different narrative structures and stylistic elements. As you read, pay attention to what draws you in. Is it the poetic prose of a classic novel, the fast-paced dialogue of a thriller, or the introspective tone of a memoir? Jot down your observations and see if any patterns emerge. Analysing the stylistic elements of your favourite authors can also be enlightening. Look at how they structure their stories, the language they use, and the way they develop their characters. This exploration helps you identify what resonates with you, laying the groundwork for your own style.

Experiment!

Experimentation is key to finding what feels natural and effective in your writing. Try your hand at writing short stories in various genres. Maybe you'll discover a hidden talent for crafting spine-tingling mysteries, or perhaps you'll find joy in creating whimsical fantasy worlds. Each genre has its unique challenges and rewards, offering new techniques to incorporate into your writing toolkit. Play with different narrative techniques as well. Write a scene from a first-person perspective, then try it in third person. Notice how the shift changes the story's intimacy and scope. This experimentation is like trying on different hats, seeing which fits best and feels the most authentic to you.

Personal influences

Reflecting on personal influences and preferences offers valuable insights into your storytelling instincts. Take some time to journal about your favourite storytelling methods. Do you prefer stories that unfold slowly, revealing layer upon layer, or do you enjoy narratives that jump right into action? Reflect on recurring themes in your personal writing. Do you often explore themes of love, loss, or transformation? These reflections can reveal underlying passions that shape your stories. Understanding these influences helps you align your writing with your authentic self, ensuring that your style is not just a mimicry of others but a true expression of your voice.

Signature style

Developing a signature style is a process that requires consistent practice. Dedicate time to daily writing exercises, treating them as opportunities to refine your craft. Set aside a quiet corner, grab your favourite pen or keyboard, and let your thoughts flow. These exercises don't have to be lengthy or polished; the goal is to cultivate a habit that keeps your creative muscles flexed. Over time, you'll notice patterns in your writing—favourite phrases, recurring rhythms, and a particular way of seeing the world. These elements coalesce into a style that is uniquely yours, a voice that readers will come to recognize and appreciate.

REFLECTION EXERCISE: JOURNALING YOUR STYLE

Spend a few minutes each day journaling about your writing experiences. What styles and genres captivate you? What narrative techniques feel most comfortable? Reflect on how your personal preferences shape your storytelling. Use these reflections to guide your exploration, honing a style that feels genuine and exciting. This practice not only enhances self-awareness but also serves as a compass, pointing you toward your unique narrative voice.

VOICE: THE WRITER'S SIGNATURE

Finding your voice

When we talk about a writer's voice, we're diving into what makes your writing uniquely yours. Think of it as the DNA of your storytelling, composed of tone, word choice, and rhythm. It's the way your sentences sway and flow, the way your words paint pictures and evoke emotions. Voice is like a fingerprint—no two are exactly alike. Take some time to read works by authors known for their distinctive voices. Consider the dark, moody tones of Edgar Allan Poe, or the whimsical, playful prose of Roald Dahl. Each author's voice is a mix of vocabulary and sentence structure that creates a certain musicality. Analysing these elements can inspire you to identify and develop your own writing voice. Finding your voice starts with recognizing the elements that characterize it. It might be the way you describe a sunset, or the way your dialogue captures the cadence of everyday speech.

Traits

Begin by crafting a list of personal writing traits. Are your sentences long and flowing, or short and punchy? Do you lean toward vivid imagery, or do you gravitate toward sparse, minimalist prose? Reflect on the themes that frequently appear in your writing. Do you often explore the complexities of human relationships, or do you prefer tales of adventure and discovery? This exercise helps you see the threads that weave through your work, highlighting the qualities that make your voice distinct. Embrace these traits—they're not just quirks; they're the heartbeat of your writing.

Authenticity

Authenticity is key to a compelling voice. It's tempting to mimic the styles of authors you admire, but the real magic happens when you embrace your own individuality. Writing personal stories or memoirs can be a powerful way to tap into your genuine voice. Share the stories that only you can tell—the ones rooted in your experiences and perspectives. These narratives often hold the raw honesty and emotion that resonate deeply with readers. It's about being brave enough to let your true self shine through your words. When you write from a place of authenticity, your voice becomes a beacon, guiding readers through your unique world. It's like inviting someone to sit with you by the fire and listen to the stories that only you can tell.

Feedback and revision

Feedback and revision are crucial in refining your voice. They're the chisels that carve your rough edges into something smooth and polished. Participating in writing workshops can offer valuable insights and constructive critique. These sessions are not about tearing down your work but about helping you see it through fresh eyes. They challenge you to push beyond your comfort zone, offering perspectives that can strengthen your voice. As you revise, pay attention to the feedback that resonates with you and aligns with your vision. Use it to refine your voice, keeping the elements that feel true to you while discarding what doesn't. Remember, every draft is an opportunity to hone your voice, to make it clearer and more resonant. Your voice is not static; it evolves with each word you write, becoming richer and more defined over time.

Exercise

Here's a little exercise to try to write a short piece, a vignette, or a scene that captures a moment personal to you. It could be about 'berries', 'childhood', or something abstract like 'serendipity'.

Then, share it in a workshop or with a trusted writing group. Listen to their responses, not for validation, but for understanding. Which parts of your voice stood out? What aspects did readers connect with? Use this feedback to polish your voice, shaping it into a tool that tells the stories only you can tell.

EXPERIMENTING WITH TONE AND PERSPECTIVE

Tone

The tone is like the mood lighting of your story—it sets the ambience and guides your readers' emotional responses. Imagine you're writing a scene where your characters are gathered around a campfire. A humorous tone might focus on the crackling fire and laughter echoing in the night, painting a picture of camaraderie and light-heartedness. In contrast, a serious tone could highlight the flickering shadows and hushed voices, creating a sense of mystery or foreboding. Tone shapes how readers perceive the story, altering their emotional engagement and drawing them deeper into the world you've crafted. Shifting from a light, comedic tone to a more serious one can transform a scene, adding layers of complexity and depth. Understanding the impact of tone allows you to manipulate it to fit the emotional arc of your narrative seamlessly.

Dimensions to storytelling

Exploring different perspectives can open up new dimensions in your storytelling. Each perspective offers a unique lens through which the reader experiences the narrative. Writing from multiple characters' perspectives can provide a richer, more nuanced understanding of your story's world. For instance, a scene described through the eyes of a wary detective will differ dramatically from that of a curious child. This shift offers fresh insights and deepens the reader's connection to the characters. Trying your hand at writing in both omniscient and limited third-person perspectives can also be enlightening. An omniscient viewpoint gives you the freedom to explore the inner workings of multiple characters, while a limited perspective allows for more focused, intimate storytelling. Experimenting with these approaches helps you determine which best serves your story's needs and enhances its themes.

Tone and genres

Tone also varies across genres, adapting to the conventions that define them. A mystery novel might adopt a suspenseful, tense tone, filled with cliffhangers and deliberate pacing to keep readers on edge. On the other hand, a romance novel might lean toward a more tender, emotive tone, focusing on the intricacies of relationships and the warmth of human connection. Adapting your tone to suit the genre ensures your story resonates with reader expectations while still allowing for creativity and originality. Comparing the tone of different genres highlights the importance of aligning your narrative voice with the themes and motifs inherent to each. This alignment creates a cohesive, immersive experience for your readers, drawing them into the genre's world.

Beyond genre conventions, tone and perspective can be powerful tools for enhancing themes and motifs within your story.

Perspectives

Shifting perspectives can reveal hidden plot layers and offer new angles on familiar situations. Imagine a story about a family reunion, told from the perspectives of different family members. Each character's viewpoint sheds light on their unique relationships and secrets, gradually weaving a complex tapestry of family dynamics. The tone can shift subtly between perspectives, reflecting each character's emotional state and the underlying themes of connection and estrangement. By carefully crafting tone and perspective, you can emphasize the themes you wish to explore, adding depth and richness to your narrative. This approach invites readers to engage more deeply with your story, uncovering its intricacies and discovering new layers of meaning as they journey alongside your characters.

CULTIVATING AUTHENTICITY IN WRITING

A seat at the table

Writing with authenticity is like offering readers a seat at your table, sharing stories that are raw, real, and resonant. It begins with drawing from personal experiences and truths. Imagine you're sitting down to write about a pivotal moment in your life—one that shaped you, left an indelible mark on your heart. Reflecting on personal milestones and challenges can breathe life into your narratives, injecting them with a sincerity that readers can't help but connect with. Whether it's the bittersweet memory of a first love or the struggle of overcoming a personal setback, these experiences provide a wellspring of material that is uniquely yours. They offer a lens through which you can explore universal themes, inviting readers to see the world through your eyes. This isn't about airing your life story, but about using your experiences to enrich the tapestry of your fiction, grounding your characters and plot in emotional truth.

Mind the predictability

Steering clear of clichés and overused tropes is crucial in maintaining this authenticity. Picture the well-worn path of a hero's journey or the predictable love triangle—these are familiar and comforting, yet they can feel stale if not handled with care. The trick is to recognize these formulaic elements and breathe new life into them. Perhaps you take a common trope and flip it on its head, offering a fresh perspective that surprises and delights. Rewriting common tropes with a unique twist not only keeps your story engaging but also respects your readers' intelligence, offering them something unexpected. It's about finding the balance between honouring the familiar and pushing boundaries, ensuring your narrative stands on its own merit. By challenging the status quo, you invite readers to see old stories through a new lens, sparking curiosity and engagement.

Vulnerability

Embracing vulnerability in storytelling can forge deeper connections with your audience. It's about peeling back the layers and allowing readers to see your characters' raw, unvarnished parts—and perhaps, by extension, parts of yourself. Writing about personal fears or failures isn't about dwelling in darkness but about illuminating the human experience in all its complexity. When you share these vulnerabilities, you invite readers to step into your characters' shoes, to feel their struggles and triumphs as if they were their own. This honesty can transform a story from mere words on a page to a living, breathing narrative that resonates on a personal level. It's about creating characters that readers can root for, empathize with, and see reflections of themselves in, fostering a sense of shared humanity.

Emotional resonance

Genuine emotional resonance is the heartbeat of a compelling narrative. It's the subtle shifts in a character's demeanour, the unspoken words that linger between lines of dialogue, and the moments of introspection that reveal inner turmoil. Crafting stories that evoke real emotions and empathy requires a keen eye for these nuances. Imagine a scene where two characters are at odds. Instead of relying on explosive confrontations, you capture the tension through averted gazes, the clench of a jaw, or the quiet resignation in a character's voice. These subtle emotional shifts can speak volumes, drawing readers into the emotional landscape of your story without resorting to melodrama. By focusing on the small, everyday moments that define relationships and experiences, you create a narrative that feels lived-in and authentic. This attention to detail ensures that your story resonates long after the final page is turned, leaving an impression that lingers in the hearts of your readers.

NURTURING CREATIVE FLEXIBILITY

Freshness

Creative flexibility is the secret sauce to keeping your writing fresh and exciting. Picture it as the ability to stretch and adapt, allowing your stories to evolve organically. This open-minded approach to writing is crucial. It means being willing to explore new ideas and techniques, stepping outside of your comfort zone to see where your creativity might lead. One way to foster this mindset is by attending writing retreats or seminars. These events are like a shot of inspiration, often introducing you to different styles and voices. Engaging with other writers and absorbing diverse perspectives can spark ideas you might never have considered on your own. Keep an open mind to the wealth of possibilities around you; it can transform your writing in unexpected and delightful ways.

Feedback is a gift

Receptiveness to feedback is another cornerstone of creative flexibility. It's about listening to what others have to say about your work, even when it challenges your perspective. This can be tough—after all, writing is deeply personal. But feedback offers invaluable insights into how your story is perceived. Consider the input from beta readers, who provide a fresh set of eyes on your draft. Their feedback can highlight areas for improvement that you might have overlooked. Use this input to revise your stories thoughtfully, embracing change as a chance to refine and strengthen your narrative. Remember, feedback is not about compromising your vision but enhancing it, creating a more compelling and polished work. Being adaptable in this way not only improves your current project but also helps you grow as a writer.

Think it? Try it!

Exploring unconventional storytelling forms is a fantastic way to shake things up and challenge your creative boundaries. Traditional narrative forms have their place, but sometimes, experimenting with different formats can breathe new life into your work. Try writing a story entirely in dialogue, letting the characters' voices drive the narrative. Or delve into the epistolary form, where letters between characters reveal the plot. Flash fiction, with its brevity and focus, can hone your ability to distil a story to its essence. Poetry, on the other hand, might allow you to play with language and emotion in a way that prose doesn't. Each of these forms offers unique opportunities for expression, encouraging you to think outside the box and expand your creative repertoire.

The balance

Balancing consistency with innovation is key to maintaining your unique voice while venturing into new creative territories. It's about holding onto what makes your writing distinctly yours while being open to blending it with new elements. Imagine maintaining your narrative style while incorporating multimedia elements, like visual art or music, into your storytelling. This fusion can create a richer, more immersive experience for your readers. The challenge lies in ensuring that these innovations enhance rather than overshadow your core voice. By striking this balance, you can explore new creative directions without losing the essence of what makes your work special.

An open mind

As writers, cultivating creative flexibility allows us to grow and adapt, keeping our work vibrant and engaging. With an open mind and a willingness to experiment, you can nurture a dynamic storytelling approach that evolves with you. Whether through feedback, unconventional forms, or new techniques, each step you take opens doors to fresh possibilities and deeper creativity. This chapter has been about embracing change and innovation, setting the stage for exploring the rich and complex worlds you will build. Next, we'll dive into creating settings and worlds that transport readers, crafting environments that are as vivid and compelling as the characters who inhabit them.

MAKE A DIFFERENCE

UNLOCK THE POWER OF SHARING

"The world needs your voice. Share it and watch how it echoes in the lives of others."

UNKNOWN

We are half way along and the story isn't over. In fact, it's just beginning.

Would you help someone just like you—dreaming of writing a novel but unsure how to start?

My mission is to make writing a novel feel possible for everyone.

But to reach other aspiring writers, I need your help.

Most people pick up books based on reviews. A few kind words from you could guide someone toward unlocking their creativity and telling their story.

Your review could inspire:

- ...one more person to finally put pen to paper.
- ...one more dreamer to believe they can write their first chapter.
- ...one more storyteller to bring their ideas to life.

It takes less than a minute and costs nothing—but it could change someone's writing journey forever.

To make a difference, simply scan the QR code below to leave a review:

If you've found joy and inspiration in this book, I know you'll love helping others discover it too. Thank you, for sharing your thoughts.

Ed Adams

CHAPTER 6
SCENE CONSTRUCTION AND PACING

The magic of dynamic scenes

Picture yourself turning the pages of a novel, completely absorbed, as each scene unfolds with vivid clarity. You can almost feel the tension in the air, hear the whispers of conflict, and sense the warmth of a sunlit room. This is the magic of dynamic scenes—those moments in a story where the world comes alive, and the narrative leaps off the page. Crafting such scenes involves more than just stringing together words; it requires intentionality, a keen sense of detail, and a balance of elements that capture the reader's imagination.

BUILDING DYNAMIC SCENES

Make every scene count

Every scene in your novel should have a clear objective, a purpose that drives the plot forward or develops your characters. Think of each scene as a stepping stone, leading your story from one point to the next. Before you start writing, ask yourself what you want to achieve with the scene. Is it to introduce a crucial plot point or highlight a pivotal change in your character's journey? Maybe it's a moment of revelation or a decision that alters the course of the narrative. By defining these objectives, you ensure that each scene serves the larger tapestry of your story. This clarity helps in identifying key plot points and understanding how a character's actions or decisions propel the narrative.

Sensory details

Using sensory details and vivid descriptions can transform a simple scene into an immersive experience. Consider the atmosphere, setting, and mood you want to convey. Imagine a scene set in a bustling coffee shop. How do the clatter of cups and the hum of conversation set the mood? Does the aroma of freshly brewed coffee evoke a sense of warmth and comfort, or perhaps nostalgia? Incorporating sensory experiences like these allows readers to step into your world, making the scene feel tangible and real. They hear the rustle of leaves, taste the salt in the air, and feel the roughness of an ancient stone wall. These details are the brushstrokes that paint the vivid picture of your narrative, drawing readers deeper into the story.

Conflict and tension

Conflict and tension are the heartbeat of any engaging scene. They provide the energy that keeps readers hooked, eagerly turning pages to see what happens next. Infuse your scenes with elements of conflict by crafting dialogue that reveals underlying tensions. Consider a heated argument between two characters: it's more than just words but a dance of power and emotion. Each line carries weight, each pause a chance for the tension to simmer. Designing actions that escalate stakes adds another layer of intrigue. Let a character's choices have consequences, pushing them closer to a breaking point. This tension propels the narrative forward, creating a sense of urgency that compels readers to keep reading.

Action and dialogue

Balancing dialogue, action, and exposition is an art form in itself. Too much of one can disrupt the flow, while too little can leave scenes feeling flat. The key is to find the right mix that keeps the narrative dynamic and engaging. Interspersing dialogue with action beats can maintain momentum, offering glimpses into a character's mindset through their movements and reactions. Perhaps a character paces the room while speaking, their agitation mirrored in their restless steps. Exposition, when used sparingly, provides necessary context without bogging down the story. It's the subtle weaving of information into the fabric of the scene, enhancing understanding without overshadowing the action.

EXERCISE: SCENE PLANNING WORKSHEET

Create a worksheet to map out your next scene.

Start by defining the scene's objective.

What are the key plot points?

What changes or decisions will your characters face?

Use this worksheet to jot down sensory details and plan how you'll incorporate conflict and tension.

Balance your elements—dialogue, action, and exposition—ensuring each serves the scene's purpose.

This structured approach will help you craft dynamic scenes that not only captivate but also resonate with your readers.

MASTERING SCENE TRANSITIONS

Thematic and emotional links

Imagine reading a novel where each scene flows into the next like a gentle river, carrying you effortlessly along the story's current. Achieving this smooth narrative flow requires creating seamless transitions between scenes. One effective method is using thematic or emotional links to connect scenes. Suppose a scene ends with a character feeling isolated after a heated argument. The next scene could open with that same character in a crowded room, yet still feeling alone. This thematic link not only provides continuity but also deepens the emotional impact, allowing the reader to carry forward the character's feelings. Transitional phrases or evocative imagery can also bridge scenes. Picture the sun setting at the close of one scene, only to rise in the next, signalling the passage of time and a new beginning. These subtle cues guide the reader, maintaining the story's rhythm while hinting at shifts in mood or tone.

Vary techniques

Transitions are not one-size-fits-all; varying your techniques can add depth and texture to your writing. Crafting abrupt transitions can heighten tension, throwing the reader into a new scene with a jolt. Imagine ending a scene on a note of suspense, only to cut sharply to another character in a different setting. This sudden shift can amplify the sense of urgency, keeping readers on their toes. Conversely, gradual transitions are perfect for reflective moments, allowing a scene to ebb gently into the next. Perhaps a character is lost in contemplation, the scene dissolving into a memory that offers insight or foreshadowing. This softer transition can enrich the narrative, providing layers that encourage readers to pause and ponder.

Cliffhangers and hooks

Ending scenes with cliffhangers and hooks is a tried-and-true method to maintain reader engagement. Consider leaving a scene with unresolved questions or looming threats. A character might discover a mysterious letter but not reveal its contents until later. This unanswered question becomes a hook, pulling readers onward. It's like dangling a carrot just out of reach, tempting them to keep turning pages to discover what happens next. The key is to ensure these hooks feel organic, not forced, so they naturally arise from the plot or character dynamics, keeping the reader's curiosity piqued without disrupting the story's flow.

Character mood and plot direction

Transitions should also reflect shifts in character mood or plot direction. As your narrative progresses, characters evolve, and the plot thickens. Transitions are an opportunity to mirror these changes subtly. If a character has just experienced a major setback, their mood might be sombre as the next scene opens, casting a shadow over their actions. Alternatively, a triumphant moment might leave a character buoyant, their optimism colouring their perspective in the following scene. These emotional shifts can be conveyed through setting descriptions, dialogue tone, or even the rhythm of your prose. By weaving these elements into your transitions, you create a cohesive narrative where each scene flows naturally into the next, mirroring the characters' journeys and the plot's evolution.

Mastering transitions

The art of transitioning between scenes is like weaving a tapestry, each thread connecting to the next in a seamless pattern. By experimenting with thematic links, varied techniques, and emotional reflections, you craft a narrative that feels both cohesive and dynamic. This mastery of transition enriches your storytelling, creating a reading experience that captivates and engages from one scene to the next.

Controlling Narrative Pacing

Imagine a rollercoaster ride where the thrill comes from its ups and downs, not just the speed. The same principle applies to narrative pacing. It's not about racing through your story but knowing when to accelerate and when to slow down. Pacing affects how readers connect with your story. A fast-paced scene can make hearts race and minds whirl, while a slower scene invites reflection and deeper emotional engagement. Recognizing the difference between these tempos is crucial. Fast-paced scenes often involve action, urgent dialogue, or pivotal plot twists. They drive the story forward and keep readers on the edge of their seats. In contrast, slow-paced scenes allow for introspection and character development, offering moments to breathe and absorb the narrative's richness.

Hone your pacing!

Adjusting the pacing to suit your narrative's needs is a skill worth honing. During action-packed sequences, short, punchy sentences can replicate the adrenaline rush of the moment. Picture a chase scene where every heartbeat counts, each sentence mirroring the protagonist's quickening pulse. Conversely, when your story calls for introspection or world-building, take your time. Expand your descriptions, letting readers linger in the details. Describe the texture of an old leather-bound book, the way sunlight filters through trees, or the quiet hum of a bustling city. These moments allow your readers to pause, reflect, and immerse themselves fully in your world. By mastering the rhythm of your prose, you guide your readers through the emotional highs and lows of your narrative, crafting an experience that resonates long after they've turned the page.

Suspense and anticipation are powerful tools in a writer's arsenal, and pacing plays a pivotal role in wielding them effectively. To build suspense, consider delaying the revelation of crucial information. Introduce a mysterious letter in one chapter but hold off on its contents until later. This delay creates a sense of intrigue, keeping readers guessing and invested in the unfolding story. Foreshadowing is another technique that builds anticipation. Sprinkle subtle hints throughout your narrative, clues that suggest future events or twists. This not only engages readers but also rewards them for their attention to detail. The anticipation of what's to come keeps them turning pages, eager to see how the pieces fit together. By strategically pacing these elements, you create a narrative that grips readers, playing on their curiosity and desire for resolution.

Create a consistent rhythm

Achieving a balanced pace throughout your narrative ensures a consistent rhythm that keeps readers engaged without overwhelming them. Alternate between high-tension and low-tension scenes to create a dynamic flow. After a nail-biting confrontation, offer a moment of calm—a scene where characters regroup, reflect, or bond. This ebb and flow prevent reader fatigue, providing a natural rhythm that mirrors the ups and downs of real life. It's like a well-composed symphony, where crescendos are followed by softer passages, allowing the audience to catch their breath before the next surge.

Balancing pacing across your story not only maintains reader interest but also enhances the emotional impact of your narrative. By carefully orchestrating this rhythm, you craft a story that captivates and resonates, leaving readers eager for more.

The key is to remember that pacing is not just about speed; it's about timing. It's about knowing when to let your story sprint and when to let it stroll. By controlling the pace, you control the reader's experience, guiding them through the emotional landscape of your story. Whether you're building tension, revealing character depth, or weaving intricate plot threads, pacing is your ally. It shapes the way readers perceive and connect with your narrative, making it an experience they won't soon forget.

BALANCING ACTION AND REFLECTION

Imagine you're in the thick of an intense scene—a chase through city streets or a heated argument that makes words feel like weapons. The adrenaline is pumping, and the stakes couldn't be higher. But once the dust settles, both characters and readers need a moment to breathe, to process the whirlwind of emotions and events. This is where reflective moments come into play, offering a counterbalance to the high-energy sequences. Following an action scene with character introspection not only provides a breather but also deepens the emotional resonance of the narrative. It's like the calm after a storm, where the air feels different, charged with the echoes of what just transpired. By blending inner monologues with external events, you allow your characters—and your readers—a chance to reflect, to understand the why behind their actions, and to grow from them.

Reflective moments are a powerful tool for character development. They invite readers into the intimate corners of a character's mind, revealing thoughts and feelings that might not be visible in the heat of action. Imagine a character grappling with the aftermath of a choice, their internal dialogue a window into their soul. Crafting these internal dialogues or using flashbacks can illuminate motivations and fears, adding layers to their personality. Perhaps a fleeting memory surfaces, reminding them of a similar situation from their past. This reflection not only enriches the character but also offers insights that can shape future decisions, creating a narrative that feels both dynamic and introspective.

Action scenes should serve a purpose beyond mere excitement. They're opportunities to advance the plot and reveal character traits, pushing characters to make choices that define them. Picture a battle scene not just as a display of skill and courage but as a moment that forces your character to choose between loyalty to a friend and duty to a cause. These choices, made under pressure, reveal true character, much like coal under heat and pressure reveals a diamond. It's in these moments that characters show their mettle, and the plot takes unexpected turns. This interplay between action and character choices creates a narrative that is both thrilling and meaningful, keeping readers invested in the outcome.

Pacing fatigue is a real risk when action scenes stretch on without relief. Even the most dedicated readers can tire if the narrative feels relentless. To prevent this, intersperse action with quieter moments, allowing both characters and readers time to recover. These pauses are like oases in a desert, offering a chance to regroup and gather strength for what lies ahead. Perhaps after a harrowing escape, your characters find themselves around a campfire, sharing stories and fears. These quieter moments provide emotional recovery, deepening relationships and setting the stage for the next wave of action. By balancing action with reflection, you create a rhythm that engages and sustains interest, much like a well-composed piece of music.

Balancing action with reflection is about creating a narrative symphony, each note carefully chosen to resonate with the reader. It's a dance between the external and internal, where every action has a reflective counterpart, and every reflection prepares the ground for future action. This balance invites readers to not only experience the thrill of the story but also to engage with its emotional core, creating a reading experience that lingers long after the final page is turned.

ENHANCING READER ENGAGEMENT THROUGH PACING

Imagine diving into a thriller where each page feels like a heartbeat, quickening as the suspense builds. That's the power of aligning pacing with reader expectations. Different genres demand different rhythms. In thrillers and action-packed tales, fast pacing is your ally. It creates a sense of urgency that keeps readers on the edge of their seats. Consider how a tightly written chase scene, with rapid dialogue and swift action, mirrors the adrenaline rush of the characters. This pace is not just about speed but about maintaining tension and excitement, ensuring your readers feel every pulse-pounding moment.

Pacing is also a tool for highlighting key themes within your story. As your narrative unfolds, there will be moments that demand the spotlight. Slowing down the pace for thematic revelations allows readers to absorb the weight of these moments fully. Picture a character discovering a long-buried truth or coming to a profound realization. By easing the pace, you give these themes the space they need to resonate. Allow readers to linger on the significance, to feel the impact of what the characters are experiencing. This slower pace can transform a simple revelation into a powerful, memorable moment.

Keeping readers engaged requires variation in pacing patterns. Imagine a story that moves at one constant speed—it risks becoming predictable, even monotonous. Introducing unexpected pacing shifts can revitalize the narrative, catching readers off guard in the best possible way. A sudden lull before an explosive event can heighten the impact, as can an unexpected burst of action in a previously calm scene. These shifts are like plot twists for pacing, keeping readers guessing and invested. They add texture and depth to your storytelling, ensuring that your narrative never feels static or stale.

Incorporating reader feedback is invaluable for refining your pacing. Readers provide a fresh perspective, often noticing pacing issues that might escape your notice. Consider workshopping scenes with a group or sharing drafts with beta readers. Their insights can pinpoint moments where the pacing feels off, whether it's dragging or rushing. Engaging with this feedback allows you to make informed adjustments, enhancing the flow and engagement of your story. It's a collaborative process, one that connects you with your audience and helps you craft a narrative that resonates with them on a deeper level.

Including a diverse range of pacing techniques in your toolkit enriches your storytelling. Whether you're crafting a high-stakes thriller or an introspective drama, understanding pacing helps you guide your readers through the emotional and thematic landscape of your story. It's a dance between speed and stillness, a balance that keeps your narrative alive and compelling. By aligning pacing with genre expectations, highlighting themes, varying patterns, and embracing feedback, you create a dynamic reading experience that captivates and engages.

In this chapter, we've explored how pacing can transform your narrative, making it engaging and resonant. As you craft your scenes, remember that pacing is more than just speed—it's about rhythm and impact. In the next chapter, we'll delve into the nuances of dialogue, uncovering how words, when spoken by your characters, can reveal their deepest truths and drive your story forward.

CHAPTER 7
OVERCOMING WRITER'S BLOCK

Imagine sitting down, ready to spill your thoughts onto the page, but instead, your mind is as blank as the screen in front of you. It's a frustrating, disheartening place, and it's known to every writer as that infamous foe—writer's block. The good news is that writer's block isn't an insurmountable wall; it's more like a fog that obscures your path. And like any fog, it can be cleared with the right tools and understanding. This chapter will help you navigate through the mist, guiding you to recognize and address the roots of your creative blocks.

IDENTIFYING THE ROOT OF CREATIVE BLOCKS

Triggers

Let's start by recognizing the personal triggers that lead to writer's block. It's like being a detective of your own mind, examining past instances where your writing ground to a halt. Was it a particular setting that stifled your creativity, or perhaps an emotional upheaval that paralyzed your pen? Try journaling about your feelings before and during these blocks. This practice can uncover patterns—maybe stress from work creeps into your writing time, or self-doubt whispers louder when tackling certain topics. By dissecting these moments, you arm yourself with knowledge, turning the unknown into something tangible that you can address.

Psychological barriers

Understanding the psychological barriers is crucial. These are the mental hurdles that stand in your way, like perfectionism or the fear of failure. Perfectionism can be a sneaky adversary, whispering that your work isn't good enough, even before it hits the page. Investigate these tendencies by reflecting on your expectations. Are they realistic, or are they set so high that they become paralyzing? Similarly, fears related to criticism or rejection can loom large, casting a shadow over your creative spirit. Acknowledging these fears is the first step toward dismantling their power. Recognize them, name them, and they become less daunting, more manageable.

Internal and external blocks

Distinguishing between internal and external factors helps clarify your path forward. Internal doubts, like those perfectionist tendencies or fear of judgment, often require a different approach than external circumstances, like a demanding job or family responsibilities. Examining work-life balance issues can reveal if your schedule leaves little room for creativity. Are there external pressures squeezing your writing time? Identifying whether your block is self-imposed or circumstantial allows you to tailor your strategies accordingly. You can't change everything in your environment but knowing where the pressure points lie can help you work around them, rather than against them.

Addressing blocks

Once you've pinpointed the roots of your block, it's time to develop a plan to address these specific barriers. Setting realistic writing expectations is a good starting point. If perfectionism is your nemesis, give yourself permission to write poorly. Drafts don't need to be perfect—they just need to exist. Set achievable goals that encourage progress over perfection. Planning for regular breaks is equally important to avoid burnout. Writing is a marathon, not a sprint; pacing yourself keeps your creativity fresh and your enthusiasm intact. These strategies aren't about lowering your standards but rather about creating a sustainable environment where creativity can thrive.

REFLECTION EXERCISE: JOURNALING YOUR BLOCKS

Insights

Spend a few minutes reflecting on a recent bout of writer's block. Write down the circumstances surrounding it and any emotions you felt. Was there a specific trigger? As you journal, seek patterns or recurring themes. Use these insights to create a personalized strategy for overcoming future blocks. This exercise helps transform vague frustrations into actionable steps, empowering you to take control of your creative process. Armed with these insights and strategies, you can face writer's block with a sense of curiosity rather than dread. Understanding what stops you from writing is half the battle won. With each block you overcome, you strengthen your resilience and deepen your connection to the stories only you can tell.

TECHNIQUES FOR REIGNITING CREATIVITY

Sparks!

Picture yourself at your desk, ready to write, but your mind feels stagnant, stuck in the same old patterns. Sometimes, all it takes to break free is a little spark. Engaging in creative exercises and prompts can be just that—an ignition to your creative engine. Start with writing prompts that push you to explore new themes or unfamiliar territories. Maybe write about a world where the sun never sets, or a character who communicates only through music. These prompts can jolt your imagination, nudging it in directions you hadn't considered before. Another powerful tool is free writing. Set a timer for ten minutes and let your thoughts spill onto the page without stopping to edit or judge. This exercise is about breaking the chains of self-censorship and letting your subconscious take the wheel. You might be surprised at the gems you uncover amidst the stream of consciousness.

Change the mood music

Sometimes, creativity needs a change of scenery, and exploring different creative mediums can offer fresh perspectives. If words aren't flowing, try expressing stories through a different form, like painting or music. Even if you don't consider yourself an artist or musician, these activities can unlock parts of your brain that writing alone might not reach. Painting can teach you about composition and colour, elements that can translate into more vivid descriptions in your writing. Music can inspire rhythm and emotion, guiding the tone and pacing of your scenes. Attending creative workshops can also expose you to new techniques and ideas. Whether it's a pottery class or an improv session, these experiences can inform your writing in unexpected ways, making your stories richer and more textured.

Hidden gold

Revisiting past projects can be a goldmine for inspiration. Remember that story you shelved three years ago or the poem that never quite came together? Dust them off and take a fresh look. Time can offer new perspectives, and you might find that what seemed like a dead end now offers new possibilities. Analyse previous drafts with an open mind, looking for elements that still resonate and those that might need reimagining. Sometimes, a minor character or subplot can bloom into its own narrative, or a discarded idea can spark an entirely new story. Reworking past projects not only breathes life into old ideas but also reminds you of your growth as a writer—what once felt insurmountable may now seem manageable.

Playfulness

Playfulness is often overlooked in writing, yet it's a powerful tool for creativity. Injecting fun and experimentation into your process can shake loose the rust and reignite your passion for storytelling. Try writing humorous short stories or poems, allowing yourself to be silly and spontaneous. This isn't about crafting the next great novel; it's about rediscovering the joy of writing. Play with language, invent quirky characters, or create absurd scenarios that make you laugh. You might also experiment with playful character sketches, imagining characters in outlandish situations or giving them whimsical traits. These exercises remind you that writing isn't just work; it's also play, a space where imagination can run wild without constraints.

Invite creativity

By embracing these techniques, you invite creativity back into your writing life. Each exercise, each playful moment, acts as a stepping stone, guiding you from stagnation to inspiration. It's about finding what excites you, what makes you curious, and following those threads wherever they lead. Creativity thrives in environments where exploration and experimentation are encouraged, where the fear of failure takes a back seat to the thrill of discovery. So, write that absurd poem, paint that chaotic landscape, and revisit those forgotten drafts. You might just find that your creativity was never lost—only waiting for a new way to express itself.

ESTABLISHING A CONSISTENT WRITING HABIT

Make it a feature

Imagine waking up each day with a sense of purpose, knowing exactly when and where you'll write. This kind of structure can transform writing from a daunting task into a natural part of your routine. It starts with setting achievable writing goals. This means defining a minimum word count goal that feels challenging yet possible. It might be 300 words a day or perhaps 1,000, depending on your lifestyle and commitments. The key is consistency. By scheduling regular writing intervals, you create a rhythm that your mind and creativity can rely on. Whether it's an hour before work or in the quiet evening hours, these writing appointments become sacred, a promise you keep to yourself.

Accountability

Accountability is your ally in building this habit. It's easy to let writing slide when no one else is watching, so finding ways to hold yourself accountable can be crucial. Consider joining a writing group where you share progress and goals. The camaraderie and shared purpose can be motivating, pushing you to meet deadlines and surpass expectations. If in-person groups aren't feasible, online communities can offer the same support. You might also use apps designed to track writing habits. These digital tools can log your daily word count, visualize your progress, and remind you of your goals. Seeing your achievements in black and white can be a powerful motivator, reinforcing the effort you've invested and the distance you've covered.

Commit!

Creating a structured writing routine is about more than just carving out time. It's about developing discipline that turns writing into a non-negotiable part of your day. Establish a consistent writing time that fits your schedule and energy levels. Maybe you're a morning person who thrives on the quiet dawn hours. Or perhaps you find your creativity peaks late at night when the world is asleep. Whatever the case, make this time yours. Treat it with the same respect and importance as any other commitment. This routine signals to your brain that it's writing time, helping you settle into the flow more easily. Over time, this discipline becomes second nature, reducing the resistance you might feel when starting a new project.

Times to celebrate

Celebrating progress and milestones is a simple yet effective way to maintain motivation. Writing a novel is a marathon, and acknowledging small wins along the way can keep your spirits high. Plan rewards for reaching word count targets or completing chapters. These rewards don't have to be extravagant—a favourite snack, a new book, or a leisurely afternoon can suffice. The act of celebrating reinforces your dedication and achievements, making the process enjoyable rather than burdensome. It's about recognizing that each step forward, no matter how small, brings you closer to your goal. These celebrations create positive associations with writing, transforming it from a task into a series of victories.

Weave into the fabric

Building a consistent writing habit is about weaving writing into the fabric of your life. It's about setting goals, finding accountability, structuring your time, and celebrating your progress. These elements work together to create an environment where creativity thrives. As you integrate writing into your daily routine, it becomes less of a chore and more of a fulfilling, rewarding practice.

MINDFULNESS PRACTICES FOR WRITERS

Mindfulness

Picture the scene: you're at your desk, but your mind is everywhere except on the task at hand. It's easy to get lost in the chaos of thoughts that swirl around, pulling you away from the page. That's where mindfulness comes into play—a tool to anchor you in the present and clear the mental clutter. Think of mindfulness as a way to sharpen your focus and calm your mind, preparing you for the writing ahead. Start with something as simple as guided meditation before your writing sessions. Even just five minutes can help settle racing thoughts and bring your mind back to center. Choose a comfortable spot, close your eyes, and focus on your breath. Let each inhale fill you with calm, each exhale release tension. This practice not only relaxes but also primes your mind for creativity, making the transition from chaos to clarity smoother.

Presence

As you settle into writing, cultivating presence in the process is key. It's about being fully engaged with your work, letting the words and ideas flow freely. One way to do this is by focusing on the sensory experience of writing. Notice the texture of the paper if you're writing by hand, the sound of keys clicking if you're typing. Feel the weight of the pen, the gentle hum of the computer. These sensory anchors help keep you grounded in the moment, gently nudging your mind back to the task when it starts to wander. By immersing yourself in these small details, you create a deeper connection with your work, fostering a sense of flow where time seems to slip away and creativity thrives.

Managing stress

Mindfulness isn't just about focus; it's also a powerful tool for managing stress and anxiety, both common companions on the writing path. Stress about deadlines, worry over whether the words will come, anxiety about how your work will be received—these can all derail the creative process. Practicing breath awareness can help manage these feelings, providing a simple yet effective way to calm nerves. Take a few moments to breathe deeply, in through the nose, out through the mouth, focusing solely on the sensation of air moving in and out. This practice slows the heart rate and reduces tension, helping you approach your writing with a clear and composed mind. It's a reminder that you have control, that you can choose to respond to stress with calm rather than panic.

Untangle those knots

Developing a mindful writing approach means integrating these practices into your routine, letting them enhance creativity and enrich the writing experience. Consider crafting reflective journal entries as part of your process. These aren't meant to be polished pieces but rather spaces to explore thoughts and emotions, to untangle the knots in your mind. Write about what's on your mind before you start your main project or reflect on what you've written afterward. This can serve as a warm-up, a way to clear the mental cobwebs and open the door to creativity. It can also be a cool-down, a chance to process and reflect on what you've created. In doing so, you give yourself the space to acknowledge your thoughts and emotions, to see them for what they are—part of the process, not obstacles to it.

Create the space for ideas

Mindfulness invites you to approach writing not as a task to be completed but as an experience to be savoured. It's about slowing down, tuning in, and letting creativity unfold naturally. By incorporating mindfulness into your writing practice, you create a space where ideas can flourish without the pressure of perfection. Let each breath guide you back to the page, each moment of awareness deepen your connection to the story you're telling.

BUILDING A SUPPORTIVE WRITING ENVIRONMENT

A space of one's own

Picture a space that's all yours, a haven where creativity flows without interruption. This is your dedicated writing space, a place where the outside world fades, and your imagination takes center stage. It's crucial that this area is comfortable and free from distractions. Consider designing a personalized writing nook that reflects your style and preferences. Whether it's a corner in your living room or a cozy spot by a window, make it yours. A clutter-free desk setup is essential, too. Clear away unnecessary items so your mind feels as open as the space around you. Organize your tools and materials within reach, ensuring everything you need to write is at hand. This simplicity invites focus, helping you slip into the writing zone with ease.

Inspiration

Inspiration fuels creativity, so surround yourself with elements that spark your imagination. Fill your writing space with motivational and creative stimuli, like inspirational quotes or art that resonates with your storytelling goals. Maybe it's a framed quote from a favourite author or an artwork that captures the essence of your story's setting. These visual cues serve as gentle nudges, reminding you of your purpose and passion when the words feel stuck. Consider changing them up periodically to keep your environment fresh and stimulating. An inspired space can be a powerful catalyst for creativity, turning mundane writing sessions into moments of discovery.

Connect

Writing can feel lonely, but it doesn't have to be. Connecting with other writers can provide invaluable support and encouragement. Participating in local writing meetups offers a chance to share experiences and challenges with fellow storytellers. If in-person gatherings aren't feasible, engaging in online writing forums can be equally beneficial. These communities offer a network of support, where you can exchange ideas, seek feedback, and celebrate victories together. Building a positive writing community not only enriches your writing journey but also offers a sense of belonging. Knowing you're not alone, that others are navigating similar challenges, can bolster your confidence and determination.

Boundaries

Protecting your writing time is as important as the writing itself. Establish clear boundaries with family and friends to ensure that your writing sessions are respected. Communicate your schedule clearly, letting them know when you'll be unavailable. This might mean setting specific times each day where interruptions are minimized or using a "do not disturb" sign to signal your writing hours. Having these boundaries in place shows respect for your craft and helps others understand the importance of your commitment. It also allows you to write without guilt or distraction, knowing that your time and space are honoured.

Mindset

Creating a supportive writing environment is about more than just the physical space. It's about fostering a mindset where creativity can thrive. You build a foundation that supports your writing endeavours by dedicating a space, surrounding yourself with inspiration, connecting with a community, and setting boundaries. These elements work together, creating an environment that nurtures your creativity and fuels your storytelling.

On the threshold of greatness

In wrapping up this chapter, remember that overcoming writer's block and building a supportive environment go hand in hand. As you design your writing space and cultivate your community, you pave the way for creativity to flourish. This foundation prepares you for the next step in your writing journey—diving into the intricate world of editing and revision.

CHAPTER 8

EDITING AND REVISION TECHNIQUES

Shiny, shiny

Imagine sitting down with a hot cup of coffee, your manuscript laid out before you and seeing it anew. It's akin to having a conversation with an old friend after a long time apart; you notice things you hadn't before, both the quirks and the charm. This fresh perspective is the magic ingredient in the art of editing. Editing isn't just about correcting typos or smoothing out grammar—it's about refining your work until it shines. It's about looking at your manuscript with a critical eye and being willing to make the changes that will transform a good story into a great one.

THE ART OF SELF-EDITING

Objectivity

Developing a critical eye for your own work is a skill that takes practice and patience. Start by approaching your manuscript with objectivity, as if you're examining it for the first time. Look for inconsistencies in plot or character that might disrupt the story's flow. Maybe your protagonist is a fearless adventurer in one scene and a timid observer in the next without a narrative reason. These inconsistencies can jar readers out of the story. Similarly, keep an eye out for repetitive language or clichés. It's easy to fall into the trap of using the same phrases repeatedly or relying on well-worn tropes. These can dilute the impact of your writing, making it feel less original. Identifying these areas for improvement is the first step in polishing your manuscript, ensuring that each sentence serves the story effectively.

The power of distance

Creating distance before revisiting your manuscript can be incredibly beneficial. Once you've completed a draft, set it aside for a while. Give yourself a break—Stephen King suggests at least six weeks. This time away allows you to return with fresh eyes, seeing your work from a new perspective. It's like watching a movie for the second time; you notice details you missed on the first viewing. During this break, engage in other creative activities or read widely. This not only refreshes your mind but also fills it with new ideas and inspiration. When you return to your manuscript, you'll be better equipped to spot areas that need work, approaching the text with clarity and insight.

Employing multiple editing passes can help you focus on different aspects of your manuscript with each read-through. In the first pass, concentrate on the big-picture elements—plot, character development, and structure. Are there plot holes that need addressing? Do character arcs feel complete? The second pass might focus on language and style, refining your prose for clarity and impact. Here, you can work on eliminating filler words and ensuring that your sentences flow smoothly. By breaking the editing process into distinct stages, you prevent overwhelm and ensure a thorough review.

Tools may help

Editing tools and resources can be valuable allies in the revision process. Software like Grammarly and ProWritingAid offer checks for grammar, style, and consistency. These tools can catch errors that might slip through even the most careful read-through, acting as a safety net for your manuscript. They highlight overused words, passive constructions, and other subtle issues you might overlook. However, remember that these tools are just that—tools. They're there to assist, not dictate. Use them to complement your instincts as a writer, ensuring that the final product maintains your unique voice.

REFLECTION EXERCISE: FRESH PERSPECTIVE

Set your manuscript aside for a month. In the meantime, engage in a different creative pursuit or immerse yourself in a genre outside your comfort zone. When you return to your manuscript, jot down any new observations or insights. Use these fresh perspectives to guide your next round of revisions, ensuring that your story evolves with clarity and depth.

STRUCTURING A REVISION PLAN

Imagine you're about to renovate a house. You wouldn't start by picking out the curtains; you'd focus on the foundation first. Revising a manuscript follows the same principle. Begin by outlining a strategy that tackles the major structural elements before diving into the nitty-gritty details. This approach ensures that your story's backbone is strong enough to support the finer touches that come later. Prioritize addressing structural changes like plot holes or character development before getting caught up in line edits or grammar tweaks. Picture your manuscript as a tapestry—first, weave the bold strokes that define the image, then refine the delicate details that complete the masterpiece.

Revision Time

Once you've identified what needs changing, it's time to carve out dedicated revision time. Revision is not something to squeeze in between daily chores or during commercial breaks. It requires focused, uninterrupted periods where you can immerse yourself in the world you've created. Consider setting a revision timeline with specific deadlines. This not only keeps you accountable but also helps you see the light at the end of the tunnel. You might designate weekends for intensive revision sessions or perhaps set aside an hour each evening. The key is consistency. Much like regular exercise strengthens muscles, regular revision sharpens your manuscript.

Breaking the revision process into manageable segments can prevent overwhelm and keep you motivated. Divide your manuscript into sections, such as chapters or scenes, and tackle them one at a time. This method allows you to focus fully on each part without feeling daunted by the whole. Start with a chapter that needs the most work or one you find particularly engaging. As you revise, concentrate on specific elements—perhaps dialogue in one pass, pacing in another. By narrowing your focus, you can address each aspect thoroughly, ensuring that nothing is overlooked. This step-by-step approach transforms the imposing task of revision into a series of achievable goals.

Tracking your progress is crucial in maintaining momentum and ensuring every area of your manuscript gets the attention it deserves. Use tools like version control or revision tracking features to monitor changes. This not only helps you keep track of what you've accomplished but also allows you to see how your manuscript evolves over time.

Revision Checklist

Maintaining a revision checklist can also be invaluable. List the areas you want to address, like plot consistency or character motivation, and check them off as you go. This not only provides a sense of accomplishment but also ensures nothing slips through the cracks. Consider keeping a journal of your revision journey, noting challenges faced and solutions found. This reflection can offer insights and inspiration as you move forward.

Finding hidden gems

As you work through your revision plan, remember that each step brings you closer to your vision. It's a process of discovery, where you unearth the hidden gems within your initial draft and polish them until they shine. Your manuscript is a living, breathing entity, and revision is the act of nurturing it to its fullest potential. Each change you make, each line you refine, draws you nearer to a story that captures the essence of your imagination.

TECHNIQUES FOR POLISHING PROSE

Polish

Crafting a vivid narrative often starts with a simple act: cutting out the clutter. Imagine your prose as a garden, where each word is a plant that needs space to grow. Too many filler words can crowd the garden, leaving no room for your ideas to breathe. Words like "very," "just," and "really" often creep into sentences, adding bulk without substance. Removing these helps streamline your language, making it clearer and more impactful. Similarly, simplifying complex sentence structures can enhance readability. Long, winding sentences may lose a reader, but shorter sentences get straight to the point. Aim for a mix of both, creating a rhythm that holds the reader's attention without overwhelming them.

It needs that swing

Rhythm in writing is like the beat in music; it keeps the reader moving through the text. Varying sentence length and structure can create a more engaging flow. Short sentences add punch and urgency, while longer ones can be used to elaborate or build suspense. Imagine your prose as a conversation with the reader, where the ebb and flow of dialogue keep them engaged. Varying the pace and structure of your sentences can guide the reader through your narrative, emphasizing key points and creating a natural, pleasing cadence. It's about finding a balance that feels right for the story you want to tell, ensuring your prose isn't just read but experienced.

Language is your palette, and words are your colours. By choosing vivid and precise language, you bring your narrative to life. Replace vague words with specific, evocative ones. Instead of saying someone is "sad," describe the "tears that glisten in their eyes" or the "weight of silence in their sigh." Strong verbs and nouns can transform a flat sentence into something dynamic and memorable. They paint a picture, drawing readers into the scene. Crafting sensory-rich descriptions allows readers to see, hear, and feel the world you've created. It's about making your story tangible, so readers aren't just observers but participants in the experience.

Consistency

Consistency in style and tone is the thread that weaves your narrative together. It's the voice that readers come to recognize and trust. Shifts in narrative voice or tense can jar readers out of the story, breaking immersion. Your narrative should feel like a seamless whole, where every part belongs to the same world. Regularly check for these inconsistencies, ensuring that your voice remains steady throughout. Think of it as staying true to your character's voice, even when the story takes unexpected turns. A coherent voice guides readers through the ups and downs, keeping them anchored in your world.

What to remove is as important as what to add

As you refine your prose, remember that editing is as much about what you remove as what you add. It's about distilling your work to its essence, where every word has purpose and impact. This process can be challenging, requiring you to make tough decisions about what stays and what goes. But it's also incredibly rewarding, as it allows your story to shine in its purest form. Through careful editing, you can transform your manuscript into something truly special, a narrative that not only tells a story but leaves a lasting impression.

INTEGRATING FEEDBACK EFFECTIVELY

Build a trust landscape of reviewers

Seeking feedback can feel like opening your home to guests—you're proud of the place, but there's always a worry they'll notice the dust in the corners. Yet, inviting others into your manuscript's world is crucial for growth. The first step is choosing who you let in. Select beta readers, critique partners, or professional editors who are not only familiar with your genre but also appreciate the nuances of your storytelling style. These trusted individuals understand the landscape you're painting and can offer insights that align with your creative vision. Think of them as guides who help navigate the terrain, pointing out paths you might have missed.

Sift with discernment

Once you've gathered feedback, it's time to sift through it with a discerning eye. Not all advice will align with your vision, and that's okay. The key is distinguishing between subjective opinions and actionable advice. If a reader suggests that a character should be more assertive, consider whether this change enhances your story's goals. Evaluate the merits of each piece of feedback: is it a personal preference, or does it highlight an area that genuinely needs improvement? This process is akin to sorting through a pile of puzzle pieces, finding those that fit seamlessly into your picture while setting aside those that don't quite align.

Brushstrokes

Incorporating feedback requires a delicate balance. You want to take advantage of helpful suggestions without compromising the story you set out to tell. It's about integrating changes that enhance your narrative while staying true to your original vision. Perhaps a reader's comment on pacing leads you to tighten a scene, increasing tension without losing your unique voice. Or maybe a suggestion on character motivation helps clarify a plot point, adding depth to your storyline. These revisions should feel like natural extensions of your narrative, each change a brushstroke that enhances the overall picture rather than altering its essence.

Open communication

Open communication with those who provide feedback is vital. Think of it as a dialogue rather than a one-way street. If a comment is unclear, don't hesitate to ask for clarification. "Can you give me an example?" or "What did you mean by that?" can open up valuable discussions. These conversations not only provide insight into the reader's perspective but also deepen your understanding of your own work. Through this exchange, you might discover nuances in your story you hadn't considered or find new ways to express your ideas more clearly.

Opportunities for growth

Integrating feedback effectively is a skill that develops with practice, much like writing itself. It involves a willingness to listen, an ability to filter advice through the lens of your vision, and the courage to make changes that strengthen your manuscript. As you work through this process, remember that every piece of feedback is an opportunity for growth, a chance to refine your story until it resonates with the clarity and impact you envisioned from the beginning.

AVOIDING COMMON EDITING MISTAKES

Don't over think it

As you navigate the editing phase, it's easy to fall into the trap of over-editing. Picture yourself endlessly tweaking each sentence, shifting commas back and forth, convinced there's always one more change to make. This can strip your manuscript of its original voice, leaving it feeling mechanical and devoid of the spark that made it unique. Recognizing when to stop editing is crucial. Trust your instincts. If a sentence captures the essence you intended, let it be. Perfection is an illusion in writing, and sometimes the raw, unpolished elements are what make your story resonate. It's about finding that balance where the essence of your narrative is preserved, even as you refine its presentation.

Big picture first

While it's tempting to focus on minor details like grammar or sentence structure, it's crucial to address the larger structural or thematic issues first. Think of your manuscript as a house. You wouldn't start with the paint before ensuring the walls are sturdy. Concentrate on the big-picture elements before diving into line edits. Is the plot consistent? Do the characters develop logically? These are the foundational questions to tackle. Once the structure is solid, you can zero in on the details with confidence. Balancing attention between the macro and micro levels of editing ensures that your story is both compelling and polished, creating a narrative that stands strong on its foundations.

Continuity

Continuity and consistency are the glue that holds your story together. Inconsistencies in plot, character, or setting can confuse readers and disrupt the immersive experience you're striving to create. Imagine a character with blue eyes in one chapter and brown in the next, or a setting that inexplicably shifts from a bustling city to a quiet village without explanation. These errors can pull readers out of the narrative, highlighting the seams in your storytelling. Using style sheets can be a lifesaver. These tools help track character traits, plot points, and setting details, ensuring continuity throughout your manuscript. By maintaining a consistent world, you allow readers to lose themselves in the story, trusting that every detail aligns with the universe you've crafted.

Trust your instincts

As you sift through feedback and edits, remember that your instincts as a writer are invaluable. Confidence in your judgment and creativity is key amidst the varying opinions you'll encounter. Feedback is important, but it's your story. Balancing external advice with your creative intent is essential. If a suggestion doesn't align with your vision, it's okay to set it aside. Trust that you know your characters and narrative best. This confidence allows you to stay true to your style, even as you refine and enhance your manuscript. It's like being the captain of your ship, steering through stormy seas with a steady hand, knowing you'll reach your destination.

The dance between refinement and creativity

Editing is a delicate dance between refinement and creativity, requiring a keen eye and a sensitive touch. By avoiding common pitfalls like over-editing, neglecting major issues, or losing continuity, you preserve the heart of your story while polishing its surface. This balance is what transforms a draft into a finished work that resonates with readers. As you continue crafting your narrative, remember that each edit is a step closer to sharing your story with the world. The process of editing is not just about correction, but about discovery and enhancement, ensuring that your voice rings clear and true through every page. As we transition to the next chapter, focus on how these refined elements will enhance every aspect of your writing, from character interactions to the worlds they inhabit.

CHAPTER 9

NAVIGATING THE PUBLISHING LANDSCAPE

A *compass*

Imagine stepping into a vast library where every book has a story, not just between its covers but in how it came to be. Each one took a unique path to find its way into a reader's hands. You might feel like a traveller without a map in the labyrinth of publishing options. But worry not because this chapter is your compass. Whether you dream of seeing your book on the shelf of a quaint bookstore or prefer the immediacy of digital platforms, understanding the publishing landscape is crucial for making informed choices about your book's future. Let's explore the routes you can take—from the traditional to the self-made and the hybrid in-between.

Traditional or Self-Publishing?

Traditional publishing often feels like the Holy Grail for many writers. It's the path where you submit your manuscript to a literary agent who, if smitten by your work, pitches it to publishing houses. With traditional publishing, a lot of the heavy lifting—editing, marketing, distribution—is taken care of by the publisher. However, this means less creative control over these aspects. The journey from book deal to release can take about two years, so patience is key. On the upside, traditional publishers offer wide distribution, including brick-and-mortar bookstores, which can be a big draw. To get started, you'll need to research publishing houses that align with your genre. Look into their catalogues, understand their submission processes, and tailor your pitches to meet their expectations. Securing a literary agent can be crucial here, as they act as the gatekeepers to these publishing giants, negotiating contracts and advocating for your work.

Self-Publishing

Self-publishing is like being the captain of your own ship. It allows you to retain control over every aspect of your book—from editing and cover design to marketing strategies. Platforms like Amazon Kindle Direct Publishing (KDP) make it accessible, offering up to 70% royalties on ebooks priced between around £2.99 and £9.99. You can launch your book as soon as it's ready, without waiting for external approval. However, self-publishing means you shoulder the responsibilities and costs, which can range from minimal to significant, depending on the services you choose. Managing publication logistics involves securing ISBNs, ensuring copyright, and deciding on distribution channels.

eBook growth is immense

While primarily online, self-published books can still reach a wide audience if marketed well. You'll need to be proactive, learning the ropes of book promotion and audience engagement. This path requires a lot of hustle, but for many, the trade-off is worth the creative freedom and potential for higher royalties.

Hybrid publishing

Hybrid publishing offers a middle ground, blending elements of traditional and self-publishing. It's like having a co-pilot on your creative journey. With hybrid publishing, you pay for services such as editing, design, and distribution, while the publisher assists with the logistics. This model provides more control than traditional publishing while offering professional support that self-publishing might lack. Costs can vary widely, so it's important to evaluate what services you need and how much you're willing to invest. Hybrid publishers often have established distribution networks, which can enhance your book's reach. However, it's crucial to research and select a reputable hybrid publisher, as this industry can attract less scrupulous operators. 'During a goldrush, sell shovels' – a useful reminder.

Creative control

When deciding which publishing path to take, consider factors like creative control, financial investment, and market reach. Traditional publishing might appeal if you seek wide distribution and are willing to relinquish some creative control. Self-publishing offers autonomy and potentially higher royalties but requires a significant personal investment in terms of time and resources. Hybrid publishing provides a blend of both, ideal for those who want support without giving up all control. Weighing these pros and cons will help you chart the best course for your book, aligning with your goals and values as a writer.

REFLECTION EXERCISE: FINDING YOUR PATH

Take a moment to reflect on what you value most in your publishing journey. Is it creative control, wide distribution, or financial reward? Write down your priorities and consider how each publishing option aligns with them. This exercise can clarify your path and help you make decisions that feel true to your vision as an author.

PREPARING YOUR MANUSCRIPT FOR SUBMISSION

'Submission Guidelines'

Imagine you're about to send your beloved manuscript out into the world. It's an exciting yet nerve-wracking moment. The key to easing those jitters is preparation, and it starts with adhering to submission guidelines. These guidelines are your roadmap, laid out by agents and publishers to streamline the submission process. Think of them as the unspoken rulebook of the publishing world. They cover everything from how to format your manuscript to the specific documents you'll need to include. Industry standards typically require your manuscript to be double-spaced with a readable font like Times New Roman. Margins should be set to one inch, and your contact information should be neatly placed on the title page. Ignoring these details can make your submission look unprofessional, and in a field where first impressions are everything, that's a risk you don't want to take. Carefully reading and following each publisher's specific instructions shows professionalism and respect for their time.

Synopsis – the narrative's heart

Now, let's talk about crafting a compelling synopsis. This is where you distil your entire novel into a single page, capturing the essence of the story without losing its spirit. The synopsis is your chance to show the depth and breadth of your narrative in a snapshot. Start by highlighting the main plot points and character arcs. It's like creating a roadmap of your story's journey from beginning to end. Avoid getting bogged down in excessive detail. Instead, focus on the elements that give your story its unique flavour. This isn't about summarizing every twist and turn but capturing the narrative's heart. Maintain narrative interest by weaving in your protagonist's motivations and the stakes they face. You want the reader of your synopsis to feel the pull of your story, to see its potential as if they were glancing at the book jacket in a bookstore.

Proposal for business case

Next up is developing a professional book proposal, especially crucial for nonfiction works. A book proposal is much more than a summary; it's a business case for your book's marketability. This document should include a market analysis, identifying who your target audience is and why they'll be eager to buy your book. Consider the current market trends and how your book fits into the existing landscape. This analysis demonstrates that you understand your audience and how to reach them. Alongside this, craft a persuasive author bio. This isn't just about listing your accomplishments but connecting them to your book's theme. What personal experiences or expertise do you bring to the table that makes you the right person to write this book? Your bio should reflect your passion and credibility, giving agents and publishers a sense of who you are beyond the words on the page.

Sample chapters

Let's not forget the importance of preparing sample chapters. These samples are your manuscript's first impression, the opening act that hooks the reader and leaves them wanting more. Selecting the right excerpts is crucial. Typically, agents and publishers prefer the opening chapters, as these set the tone for the entire book. You want to choose chapters that showcase your writing style and storytelling ability. Edit these sections meticulously for maximum impact and clarity. The goal is to create a seamless reading experience that draws the reader in from the very first line. Pay attention to pacing, character introductions, and scene-setting. Every element should work in harmony to offer a glimpse of the world you've built and the journey your characters will undertake.

EXERCISE: CRAFTING YOUR SUBMISSION PACKAGE

Submission package checklist

Create a checklist for your submission package. Include items like the manuscript formatted to industry standards, a one-page synopsis, a professional book proposal, and polished sample chapters. As you prepare each element, tick it off the list. This exercise not only ensures you've covered all bases but also helps reduce anxiety by visualizing your progress.

BUILDING AN AUTHOR PLATFORM

Digital presence

Picture this: your words have the power to reach readers across the globe, and all you need to start is an internet connection. Building an author platform is about crafting a digital presence that not only showcases your work but also connects you with readers and industry professionals. It starts with creating an author website or blog. Think of this space as your virtual home, where visitors can learn about you, your writing, and your books. A well-designed website should be easy to navigate, with sections for your biography, books, blog posts, and contact information. It's your hub for sharing updates and engaging with your audience, so make it a reflection of your personality and writing style.

Engagement

Social media platforms (ever changing!) play a significant role in expanding your reach. Each platform offers unique ways to connect with your audience. The key is to choose platforms that align with your strengths and interests, and to maintain a consistent presence. Regularly post content that resonates with your audience, whether it's writing tips, book recommendations, or behind-the-scenes glimpses of your writing process.

Engagement is the heart of a successful author platform. It's not enough to have followers; you need to interact with them to build a community around your work. Consider hosting live Q&A sessions or virtual book clubs to foster direct dialogue with your readers. These events allow you to discuss your books, answer questions, and share insights into your writing journey. Encourage readers to leave reviews and provide feedback on your work. This not only increases your book's visibility but also helps you understand what resonates with your audience. Remember, engagement is a two-way street; take the time to listen to your readers and respond thoughtfully to their comments and messages.

Content Marketing

Content marketing is a powerful tool for increasing your visibility and establishing authority within the writing community. Consider writing articles or guest posts for genre-specific blogs to showcase your expertise and reach new audiences. Sharing your knowledge and experiences can position you as a thought leader and attract more readers to your work. Additionally, explore multimedia content like podcasts or video blogs. These formats allow you to connect with your audience in a more personal way, offering insights into your writing process or discussing topics related to your books. Content marketing is about creating valuable, shareable content that draws people in and keeps them coming back for more.

Networking

Networking is another crucial element of building your author platform. Connecting with other writers and industry professionals can open doors to new opportunities and collaborations. Attend writing conferences and workshops to meet like-minded individuals and learn from experts in the field. These events provide a wealth of knowledge and can help you stay updated on industry trends. Joining professional writing associations offers additional networking opportunities and resources to support your career growth. Remember, building a network is about forming genuine connections, so approach these interactions with openness and enthusiasm.

INTERACTIVE ELEMENT: NETWORKING CHECKLIST

Create a networking checklist to keep track of industry events, writing conferences, and associations that interest you.

Set goals for each event, such as meeting a certain number of new people or attending specific workshops. Use this checklist to plan your networking activities and ensure you're making the most of every opportunity.

As you build your author platform, remember that authenticity is key. Be genuine in your interactions and let your personality shine through. Your platform should reflect who you are as a writer and offer value to your audience. Whether you're sharing insights, engaging with readers, or connecting with fellow writers, approach each interaction with enthusiasm and sincerity.

Your platform is more than just a promotional tool; it's a community where you can share your passion for writing and connect with others who appreciate your work.

NAVIGATING LITERARY AGENTS AND QUERIES

A word about agents – you decide

The phrase "selling shovels in a gold rush" refers to the idea that people who sell supplies to prospectors during a gold rush can make more money than the prospectors themselves. This saying originated after the California Gold Rush of the mid-19th century, when it became clear that most prospectors didn't strike it rich.

Instead, the people who made money were those who sold supplies like shovels, pickaxes, tents, dry goods and jeans (e.g. famously Levis) to the prospectors. The term "pick-and-shovel play" is an investment strategy that refers to buying stock in a supplier to an industry instead of the company that produces the finished good.

Statistics

There are many more self-published books than books represented by agents:

- Number of books published: There are an estimated 10–20 times more self-published books than traditionally published books each year.
- E-book sales: Self-published authors account for more than half of e-book unit sales and over a third of e-book retail revenue.

It is generally not possible to find an agent to represent a novel that has already been self-published. However, a self-published novel with good sales and reviews can help convince an agent or publisher that you have a ready-made platform.

Similarly, someone with 'Authority' in a field is more likely than an 'unknown' or 'Non-Authority-Figure'.

Landing a book deal is difficult. Some say the odds of getting a traditional publishing deal are as low as one in a million, while others say they are as high as 23%.

Agents

Imagine this: you've poured your heart into your manuscript, and now it's time to share it with the world. Enter the literary agent, your potential ally in the publishing world. Agents are like the backstage pass to the big show. They're the ones who can open doors to publishing houses, negotiate contracts, and advocate for your work. Their role is not just about selling your manuscript but also about guiding your career. Finding the right agent is akin to finding a partner who believes in your vision as much as you do. Start by identifying reputable agents who specialize in your genre. This ensures they have the right connections and understanding of the market you're aiming for. Dive into research by reading up on their submission preferences and track records. Look at who they've represented and the types of deals they've secured. This will give you insight into whether they're a good match for your work.

Query letter

Once you've pinpointed potential agents, the next step is crafting a query letter that stands out. Think of this letter as your manuscript's first impression, the hook that reels an agent in. Begin with a strong opening that captures the essence of your story or highlights your unique selling point. This could be a compelling line or an intriguing question that piques curiosity. Then, move on to summarizing your plot succinctly. It's a balancing act between providing enough detail to intrigue and keeping it concise to maintain interest. Highlight the main plot points and give a taste of the protagonist's journey. The goal is to leave the agent wanting more, eager to read your manuscript. Remember, your query letter is not just about the story, but also about you as a writer. A brief bio can add a personal touch, showing your passion and connection to the material.

Submission Process

The submission process can be daunting, but organisation is your friend. Keeping track of your queries is vital. Consider maintaining a query submission log. This can be as simple as a spreadsheet listing the agents you've contacted, the dates of submission, and any responses you receive. This log not only helps you stay organized but also provides a clear picture of where your manuscript stands. It's easy to lose track when you're sending out multiple queries, but having a system in place ensures you're always on top of things. It also helps you avoid the faux pas of querying the same agent multiple times. Patience is key here. Responses can take weeks or even months, and having a log can help manage expectations during this waiting period.

Handling rejections

Rejections are a harsh reality in the writing world, but they're also an opportunity for growth. It's easy to take them personally, but remember, they're often not a reflection of your talent. Instead, view them as feedback. Some agents might provide specific reasons for their decision, offering valuable insights. Use this feedback to refine your query letter or manuscript. Revisiting and revising your query based on agent responses can be beneficial. Sometimes a tweak here or a shift in emphasis there can make all the difference. Keep in mind that every rejection brings you one step closer to finding the right agent who truly resonates with your work. Resilience in the face of rejection is what sets successful writers apart. It's about learning, adapting, and continuing to push forward with your writing ambitions.

It is not an end goal

As you navigate this chapter, remember that finding an agent is not the end goal but a step toward sharing your story with the world. Each query sent and each response received is part of the larger process of bringing your book to life. As we wrap up this chapter, let's look ahead to understanding what comes next—a deeper dive into the marketing strategies that will help your book find its audience and truly make its mark.

CHAPTER 10

MARKETING YOUR NOVEL AND BUILDING AN AUDIENCE

Setting sail

Imagine your novel as a beautifully crafted ship, ready to set sail across the vast ocean of readers' minds. The excitement of writing it is the wind in your sails, but without a map —a solid marketing strategy—how will it find its way to eager readers? Marketing your book is that map, guiding you from unknown author to beloved storyteller. It's a journey of discovery, not just for your book, but for you as a writer, as you learn to connect with the very people who will cherish your story.

Sailing to where?

To start, defining your target market is crucial. Think of your ideal reader as a character in your story—what do they look like, what are their interests, and where do they spend their time? Conducting market research helps pinpoint these reader demographics, offering insights into their age, gender, reading habits, and even the genres they love. This knowledge allows you to create reader personas, fictional representations of your ideal readers, which can guide your marketing tactics. For instance, if your novel is a suspenseful thriller, your target market might include adults who enjoy gripping narratives and complex characters. Knowing your audience helps tailor your marketing efforts, ensuring your message resonates with those most likely to appreciate your work.

Being smart again

Once you've identified your audience, setting clear marketing goals is your next step. These goals should be SMART—Specific, Measurable, Achievable, Relevant, and Time-bound. If you aim to increase book sales by a certain percentage within six months or expand your newsletter subscriber list by a set number, you need a clear plan to get there. These objectives not only provide direction but also allow you to measure success and adjust tactics as needed. Having a goal like "sell 500 copies in six months" or "gain 200 new subscribers" gives you a concrete target to strive for, transforming vague aspirations into actionable steps. This strategic approach keeps your efforts focused, ensuring every action you take moves you closer to achieving your goals.

Developing a multi-channel marketing plan is essential for reaching a broader audience. This involves using various platforms and media, from traditional outlets like newspapers and radio to digital platforms like blogs and social media. Combining these approaches maximizes your reach and appeal, ensuring you connect with diverse segments of your audience. Organic marketing, such as engaging with readers on social media, can build a loyal following, while paid advertising, like social media ads or sponsored blog posts, can boost visibility and attract new readers. The key is to find the right balance, leveraging the strengths of each channel to support your overall strategy. This approach ensures that, whether through an eye-catching social media post or a compelling radio interview, your novel finds its way into the hearts of readers.

Measure it!

Measuring and adjusting your marketing efforts is like fine-tuning an instrument. You need to track results and adapt strategies based on performance data, ensuring you hit the right notes with your audience. Using analytics tools helps monitor campaign success, providing insights into what works and what doesn't. Perhaps a particular social media post garnered more engagement than others, or a blog review led to a spike in sales. By analysing these metrics, you can refine your approach, focusing on tactics that yield the best results. Adjusting strategies based on reader engagement metrics ensures your efforts remain effective and relevant, allowing you to respond to changes in the market or audience preferences. This ongoing process of evaluation and adaptation ensures your marketing remains dynamic, responsive, and ultimately successful in connecting your novel with its intended audience.

VISUAL ELEMENT: MARKETING STRATEGY FLOWCHART

Strategy

Create a simple flowchart to visualize your marketing strategy. Start with your target market at the top, followed by marketing goals, channels, and measurement tools. This tool can help you see the process at a glance, making it easier to adjust as needed.

Embarking on this marketing voyage requires creativity, patience, and a willingness to adapt. As you chart your course, remember that marketing is not just about selling books; it's about building lasting relationships with readers who will cherish your stories.

LEVERAGING SOCIAL MEDIA AND ONLINE PRESENCE

Stepping into the vibrant world of social media can feel like walking into a bustling city, each platform a different neighbourhood with its own vibe and community. Choosing the right platforms for your audience is crucial. Imagine Instagram as a gallery where visual storytelling takes centre stage. It's perfect for sharing captivating images, from book covers to behind-the-scenes snapshots of your writing process. Readers love seeing the intimate corners of an author's creative world, where the magic happens. If you're crafting a visually rich fantasy or an evocative romance, such that shared glimpses might be your stage. Meanwhile, social media is like the city square, buzzing with real-time interaction. Here, you can engage in conversations, share quick updates, and join trending discussions. It's a place to connect instantly with readers and fellow writers, exchanging ideas in snappy, engaging bursts.

And think about how to capture those interested readers in a mailing list. They become your fan-base.

Engagement – the lifeblood

Creating engaging and consistent content is the lifeblood of your online presence. It's about opening a window into your world, inviting readers to peek inside. Share the journey of your writing process—those late-night brainstorms or the joy of nailing a tricky chapter. This transparency builds a connection, letting readers feel like part of your creative adventure. Visual content, like character sketches or artwork, adds another layer. It gives readers a tangible connection to your story, turning abstract characters into vivid personalities. Consistency is key here; regular updates keep your audience engaged, building anticipation for what's next. It's like feeding a fire, each post a log that keeps the flames alive, warming the bond between you and your audience.

Building a brand around your author persona is about more than just aesthetics; it's about crafting an identity that resonates with your voice and values. Think of it as your signature, the essence of who you are as a writer. Start with a memorable author tagline or slogan—something that encapsulates your style or the themes you explore. This becomes your literary calling card, a line that readers associate with your work. Your social media profile should reflect this identity, seamless and cohesive, from the colours and fonts to the images and messaging. It's not about creating a persona but revealing the authentic you, the writer behind the words. This authenticity fosters trust and recognition, making readers feel they know you, not just your books.

Meaningful interaction

Interacting meaningfully with followers transforms casual readers into dedicated fans. Engagement is more than just a numbers game; it's about building genuine connections. Respond to comments and messages promptly, showing that you value their time and thoughts. These interactions might seem small, but they're the bricks that build the foundation of a loyal readership. Hosting interactive polls or Q&A sessions invites readers into a dialogue, turning a one-sided story into a collaborative experience. It's like hosting a dinner party where everyone's voice is heard, each contribution adding flavour to the conversation. This participatory approach not only deepens engagement but also provides insights into what your audience loves and hopes to see more of.

In this digital age, your online presence is a powerful tool, a bridge connecting you to readers across the globe. It's where your voice can echo, where you can share not just your stories but your journey, your struggles, and your triumphs. Social media, when used thoughtfully and authentically, becomes more than a platform—it becomes a community, a place where readers not only discover your work but become part of its world. With the right approach, this digital space transforms into a vibrant ecosystem, alive with interaction and creativity, where every post, tweet, or image is a thread that weaves readers closer into the fabric of your storytelling universe.

ENGAGING WITH READERS AND BUILDING A COMMUNITY

Sharing

Imagine a place where your readers gather, not just to devour your stories but to share their thoughts, ideas, and excitement. This is the heart of building a community—a space where readers feel connected to you and each other. Think about creating a dedicated reader group on platforms like Facebook. It's like hosting a book club, but with people from all over the world. Here, you can encourage discussions about your book's themes, characters, and plot twists. It's where readers can dive deeper into the story, share favourite moments, and even speculate about what might happen next. This kind of engagement transforms casual readers into a community of fans who are invested in your work and eager to discuss it with others.

Exclusives

Offering exclusive content and incentives can be a game-changer. Imagine giving your readers a little something extra, something that makes them feel special. You could share bonus chapters or short stories that delve into a character's backstory or explore different points of view. These treats deepen their connection to your world and give them more to talk about in their groups. Hosting giveaways or contests exclusively for your community members can also boost engagement. Whether it's a signed copy of your book or unique merchandise, these incentives can create buzz and excitement. They show your appreciation, making readers feel valued and encouraging them to stick around for more.

Encouraging participation

Encouraging reader participation and feedback is another key aspect of community building. Inviting your readers to take part in the creative process can be incredibly rewarding for both you and them. Consider conducting reader surveys for future projects. These surveys can provide valuable insights into what your audience loves, what they want more of, and even what they'd like to see differently. You might also invite beta readers from your community to provide feedback on upcoming works. This not only makes readers feel involved but also gives you constructive criticism to refine your story. It's a win-win situation, where readers feel heard and you gain perspectives that enhance your writing.

Recognition of the readers

Recognizing and celebrating reader contributions is essential for strengthening the bonds within your community. Acknowledge their support and creativity by featuring fan art or reader reviews on your social media or website. These features highlight the talent and passion of your readers, making them feel seen and appreciated. Hosting appreciation posts or events is another way to celebrate your community. It could be as simple as a shout-out to active members or an online event where you interact directly with your readers. These gestures foster loyalty and gratitude, reinforcing the connections that make your community vibrant and engaging.

INTERACTIVE ELEMENT: READER FEEDBACK SURVEY TEMPLATE

Create a simple survey template with questions about favourite characters, plot twists, and themes. Share it with your community as a way to gather insights and show that you value their opinions.

HOSTING SUCCESSFUL BOOK LAUNCHES

Launches

Picture this: the day your book finally steps out into the world. It's a moment that deserves celebration, not just for you but for the readers eagerly awaiting your story. Planning a memorable launch event is like setting the stage for this grand debut. You have options aplenty: host a themed launch party that immerses guests in your book's universe or organize a webinar that invites readers from all corners of the globe. Themed events, whether in-person or virtual, can transport attendees into the world you've so carefully crafted. Think about incorporating interactive elements like quizzes or games related to your book's plot or characters. These activities are fun and engaging, and they also deepen the connection between your readers and your story, transforming a simple launch into an unforgettable experience.

Book signings

Getting the community involved can amplify your book's reach. Consider coordinating with local bookstores and libraries, venues that are often eager to support authors. Organizing book signings or readings at these locations can open the door to new audiences, people who might stumble upon your event and become intrigued by your story. Collaborating on local author panels or events invites you into a broader conversation, positioning you among fellow writers and engaging potential readers who are already invested in the literary world. These partnerships not only boost your visibility but also create a sense of local support and camaraderie. Each event is a chance to forge connections, turning curious attendees into lifelong fans.

Influencers

In the digital age, media and influencers wield significant power in amplifying a book's reach. Drafting press releases for local media outlets is a way to spread the word beyond your immediate network. A well-crafted press release can capture the interest of journalists, leading to coverage that can draw in readers who might otherwise have missed your book. Partnering with book bloggers or Instagram influencers further expands your reach. These individuals often have dedicated followings who trust their recommendations. By collaborating with them, you tap into these networks, gaining exposure to engaged audiences who are eager for new reads. Building relationships with influencers can create a ripple effect, where their enthusiasm for your book sparks interest across their platforms.

Countdown and promotion

Creating a launch countdown and promotional campaign is about building anticipation and momentum leading up to your book's release. Countdown graphics and teasers shared across your platforms can generate excitement, reminding your audience of the upcoming launch. Consider running pre-order promotions or offering discounts as a way to incentivize early purchases. These strategies not only boost initial sales but also create a sense of urgency and exclusivity. Readers love feeling like they're part of something special, and a well-timed campaign can make your book a must-have item. As the launch date approaches, these efforts culminate in a swell of enthusiasm, ensuring your book enters the world with the fanfare it deserves.

SUSTAINING LONG-TERM READER ENGAGEMENT

Imagine your readers as guests at an ongoing party, where the conversation is lively, the connections are genuine, and there's always something new to discover. Keeping readers engaged over the long haul requires maintaining regular communication, much like nurturing any relationship. Consider sending monthly newsletters filled with updates about your latest projects, insights into your writing process, or even snippets from your current work. These newsletters act as a friendly nudge, reminding readers of your presence and keeping them excited about what's to come. Hosting regular live chats or virtual meetups offers another way to maintain this connection. These gatherings provide a platform for real-time interaction, where you can discuss recent works, answer questions, and perhaps share sneak peeks of future endeavours. It's an opportunity to engage with your readers on a personal level, making them feel valued and involved in your creative journey.

Keeping content fresh and relevant is key to sustaining interest. Readers are naturally curious and providing them with new material keeps that curiosity alive. Consider releasing serialized stories or novellas between your major projects to bridge the gap and maintain momentum. These shorter works can explore different facets of your universe or introduce new characters, offering readers something to savour while they wait for your next big release. Personal reflections or writing tips shared through blog posts or social media can also engage your audience. By opening a window into your creative world, you invite readers to connect with you not just as an author but as a person. This transparency builds trust and keeps your readers invested in your journey, eager to discover what you'll share next.

Loyalty

Encouraging reader loyalty through reward programs can significantly enhance engagement. Imagine a reader loyalty club, a community within your community, offering exclusive perks to its members. These perks could include early access to new releases (Advanced Reader Copies), special merchandise, or even personalized notes of thanks. Such initiatives provide tangible rewards for dedication, reinforcing the bond between you and your most enthusiastic supporters. They also create a sense of belonging, where members feel like they're part of an inner circle, privy to exclusive content and insights. This approach not only fosters loyalty but also turns readers into advocates, eager to share their experiences with others. It's a win-win situation, where both you and your readers benefit from the strengthened relationship.

Evolving literary landscape

Adapting to changing reader interests and trends is crucial for staying relevant. The literary landscape is ever evolving, with new genres and themes capturing the public's imagination. Keeping a finger on the pulse of these trends can help you align your content strategy with current preferences, ensuring your work remains appealing. Monitoring industry developments and reader feedback provides valuable insights into emerging interests. Perhaps a particular genre is gaining popularity, or a new theme resonates with audiences. Adjusting your approach to incorporate these elements can reinvigorate your work and keep it fresh. This adaptability demonstrates your willingness to evolve alongside your readers, maintaining their engagement and fostering long-term interest.

Sustaining reader engagement is about more than just maintaining contact; it's about creating a vibrant, dynamic relationship that grows over time. By nurturing communication, delivering fresh content, rewarding loyalty, and staying attuned to By understanding trends, you build a foundation for lasting connections. This chapter has explored the many ways to engage your readers for the long term, ensuring they remain enthusiastic and invested in your work. As you continue to develop these strategies, remember that your readers are not just an audience—they're partners in your creative adventure.

CONCLUSION

The path travelled

As we wrap up our journey together, let's take a moment to revisit the path we've travelled in this book. We've walked through the intricate steps of turning a novel idea into a best-seller. From laying the foundation of your writing vision to mastering plot development, every chapter aimed to equip you with the tools to transform your story from concept to completion.

Write with intention and clarity

Reflecting on the core vision of this book, writing with intention and clarity stands at the forefront. It's been about guiding you through the creative process with purpose, helping you craft stories that resonate and leave an impact. Remember, your journey as a writer is not just about reaching the finish line; it's about understanding the power of your narrative and the unique voice you bring to the literary world.

Skills

Throughout the chapters, we've covered essential skills like developing compelling plots, creating memorable characters, and building immersive worlds. You've learned to find your unique voice and navigate the challenges of the publishing landscape. These key takeaways are not just tools; they're stepping stones that will help you achieve your writing goals and bring your stories to life.

Traversing the hurdles

We've also addressed some of the common hurdles aspiring writers face. Dealing with writer's block, understanding the

REFERENCES

How to Create Your Writer's Vision Statement https://marisamohi.com/writers-vision-statement/

Embracing the Impact of Personal Experiences on Your ... https://www.writersdigest.com/write-better-nonfiction/embracing-the-impact-of-personal-experiences-on-your-writing

Identifying Your Book's Target Audience https://www.writersdigest.com/writing-advice/identifying-your-books-target-audience

How to Set SMART Writing Goals for 2024 https://writers.com/smart-writing-goals

How to Create a Compelling Story Arc - Jerry Jenkins https://jerryjenkins.com/story-arc

Character-Driven Vs Plot-Driven Stories: A Guide https://jerichowriters.com/character-driven-vs-plot-driven-stories/

Symbolism in Literature: What Symbolism Is, and How to ... https://writers.com/what-is-symbolism-in-literature

11 Plot Pitfalls—and How to Rescue Your Story From Them https://www.writersdigest.com/improve-my-writing/rescue-your-story-from-plot-pitfalls

How to Create a Character Profile: A Step-by-Step Guide ... https://jerryjenkins.com/character-profile/

9 Proven Steps for Memorable Character Development https://jerryjenkins.com/character-development/

50 Examples of Dialogue to Inspire Writers https://thejohnfox.com/2021/01/50-examples-of-dialogue-that-writers-should-learn-from/

Character Motivation: All You Need To Know https://jerichowriters.com/character-motivation-all-you-need-to-know/

How to Bring Your Writing to Life with Sensory Language https://www.novlr.org/the-reading-room/how-to-bring-your-writing-to-life-with-sensory-language

The Synergy of Character, Plot, and Setting https://docmckee.com/fiction/the-synergy-of-character-plot-and-setting/

How to develop a social structure for your fictional world https://www.firstdraftpro.com/blog/how-to-develop-a-social-structure-for-your-fictional-world

Realism vs. Fantasy in Fiction: Balancing Believability and ... https://charliiapp.com/realism-vs-fantasy-in-fiction-balancing-believability-and-imagination/

How to Find Your Voice in Writing: 5 Steps to Developing a ... https://www.masterclass.com/articles/how-to-find-your-voice-in-writing

Voice in Literature: Definition & Examples https://www.supersummary.com/voice/

Navigating Perspectives: The Art of Point of View in ... https://www.hireawriter.us/storytelling/navigating-perspectives-the-art-of-point-of-view-in-story telling

10 Tips to Avoid Clichés in Writing https://www.writersdigest.com/whats-new/10-tips-to-bypass-cliche-and-melodrama

How to Structure Scenes in Your Story (Complete Series) https://www.help ingwritersbecomeauthors.com/how-to-structure-scenes/

How to Create Tension in a Story: 8 Simple Steps https://www.nownovel.com/blog/create-tension-writing/

Mastering Scene Transitions https://theeditorsblog.net/2010/12/16/master ing-scene-transitions/

How to Master Narrative Pacing: 7 Tips to Help Pace Your ... https://www.masterclass.com/articles/how-to-master-narrative-pacing

Writing motivation to help you work around emotional ... https://marionroach.com/2020/06/writing-motivation-workarounds-for-those-emotional-trig gers/

*14 Best Writing Exercises to Help You Smash Writer's Block to ...*https://www.lucidhousepublishing.com/blog/14-best-writing-exercises-to-help-you-smash-writers-block-to-bits

Mindfulness Techniques for Writers https://rachelgrosvenorauthor.com/mind fulness-techniques-for-writers/

Creating An Environment Conducive To Writing https://www.autocrit.com/editing/library/creating-an-environment-conducive-to-writing/

How to Edit a Novel: The Foolproof 9-Step Book ... https://thewritepractice.com/how-to-edit-a-novel/

Notes from Stephen King's "On Writing" 07: The Revision ... https://www.tumblr.com/writing-prompts-for-friends/613924827656585216/notes-from-stephen-kings-on-writing-07-the

Use the Right Grammar Tools for Writing Your Novel https://www.getnovel ize.com/grammar-tools

The Importance of Beta Readers - Publishers Weekly https://www.publisher sweekly.com/pw/by-topic/authors/pw-select/article/91243-the-impor tance-of-beta-readers.html

Self-Publishing vs Traditional Publishing: A Thorough Side-by ... https://www.tiffanyhawk.com/blog/self-publishing-vs-traditional-publishing-a-stone-cold-sober-analysis

Start Here: How to Write a Book Proposal ... https://janefriedman.com/start-here-how-to-write-a-book-proposal/

The 16 BEST Self-Publishing Companies of 2024 https://blog.reedsy.com/best-self-publishing-companies/

List of Literary Agents 2024-2025 | Agents Looking for New ... https://literaryagencies.com/list-of-literary-agents/

Top Book Marketing Strategies for 2024: How to Promote Your ... https://spines.com/top-book-marketing-strategies-for-2024/

The Right Way to Use Social Media for Authors https://foxprinteditorial.com/2023/07/13/the-right-way-to-use-social-media-for-authors/

How to Build Your Author Platform https://jerryjenkins.com/how-to-build-your-author-platform/

How to Do Influencer Outreach for Your Book Promotion https://booklaunchers.com/influencer-outreach-book-promotion/

ED ADAMS NOVELS

TRIANGLE TRILOGY

- T1 **The Triangle** Dirty money? Here's how to clean it. Money laundering
- T2 **The Square** Weapons of Mass Destruction – don't let them get on your nerves. A viral nerve agent being shipped by terrorists and WMDs.
- T3 **The Circle** The desert is no place to get lost. In the Arizona deserts, with the Navajo; about missiles stolen from storage.

COSY TRILOGY

- T4 **Cosy** Cosy crime and thrills in Devon
- T5 **Church** Rain down on me- This is no ordinary church.
- T6 **Dark** Control is power, until it slips
- T7 **Secrets** The Cosy crime and thriller collection

ARCHANGEL COLLECTION

- A1 **Archangel** Sometimes I am necessary. Icelandic-born, Russian trained agent Christina Nott learns her craft.
- A2 **Raven** An eye that sees all between darkness and light. Big business gone bad and being a freemason won't absolve you.
- A3 **Card Game** The power of Tarot whilst throwing oil on a troubled market
- A5 **Play On, Christina Nott** Money, Mayhem, Manipulation. Christina Nott, on Tour for the FSB
- A6 **Corrupt** Parliamentary corruption. Trouble at the House

- A7 **Sleaze** Autos, Politics, Gstaad

BIG SCIENCE

- B1 **Coin** Get rich quick with Cybercash – just don't tell GCHQ
- B2 **An Unstable System** Creating the right kind of mind
- B3 **The Watcher** We don't need no personal saviours here. From the Big Bang to the almighty Whimper
- B4 **Jump** Some kind of future.
- B5 **Pulse** Sci-Fi dystopian blood management with nano-bots. Want more? Just stay away from the edge
- E1 **Edge** World end climate collapse and sham discovered during magnetite mining from Jupiter's moon Ganymede.
- E2 **Edge Blue** Endgame, for Earth – unless?
- E3 **Edge Red** Museum Earth an artificially intelligent outcome – unless?

MASTER COLLECTIONS

- C1/T4 **The Ox Stunner** The Triangle Trilogy – thick enough to stun an ox. Triangle, Circle, Square in one heavy book. all feature Jake, Bigsy, Clare, Chuck Manners
- C2/A4 **Magazine Clip** First three Archangel novels
- C3/A8 **Ignoble** Corrupt and Sleaze omnibus – double album
- C4/B7 **The Dealer** Jump, Pulse and Rage Collection
- C5/E4 **Edge of Forever** Edge Trilogy
- C6/T7 **Secrets** The Cosy crime and thriller collection

Printed in Great Britain
by Amazon

52908096R00099